HEAR THE WHISTLE BLOWING

RAILROADING IN THE COAL REGION

J. R. LINDERMUTH

SUNBURY
P R E S S

Mechanicsburg, PA USA

Published by Sunbury Press, Inc.
Mechanicsburg, Pennsylvania

www.sunburypress.com

For information about special discounts for bulk purchases, please contact Sunbury Press Orders Dept. at (855) 338-8359 or orders@sunburypress.com.

To request one of our authors for speaking engagements or book signings, please contact Sunbury Press Publicity Dept. at publicity@sunburypress.com.

ISBN: 978-1-62006-840-3 (Trade Paperback)

Library of Congress Control Number: 2018959193

FIRST SUNBURY PRESS EDITION: October 2018

Product of the United States of America
0 1 1 2 3 5 8 13 21 34 55

Set in Bookman Old Style
Designed by Crystal Devine
Cover by Terry Kennedy
Edited by Erika Hodges

Continue the Enlightenment!

For my railroading ancestors

*I've been working on the railroad
All the live-long day.
I've been working on the railroad
Just to pass the time away.*

*Can't you hear the whistle blowing,
Rise up so early in the morn;
Can't you hear the captain shouting,
"Dinah, blow your horn!"*

CONTENTS

PROLOGUE

Some of my earliest memories are the melancholy wail of a steam engine's horn, the clackety-clack of iron wheels against the rails, and the sharp scent of creosote on the cross ties.

I grew up in a Pennsylvania railroading family. My dad, my grandfather, my great-grandfather, and other family members were railroaders. The railroad brought John Samuel Lindermuth Jr., my great-grandfather, from his birthplace of Schuylkill Haven, Schuylkill County, to Shamokin, Northumberland County, where it took his life. That did not sway his sons from following in his footsteps to a variety of jobs on the Reading line.

Born in the Alaska mine patch, Mount Carmel Township, Robert Lindermuth, my grandfather, spent most of his working life on the railroad. His older brother, Charles Samuel, was engineer of the train that killed their father. Another brother, Edward, worked on the railroad until his early death as a result of tuberculosis. Their sister, Elizabeth, married Alfred Trout, who retired as a locomotive engineer on the Lehigh Valley Railroad.

My grandfather began work with the Reading as a machinist and was transferred to the passenger car cleaning department after being injured in an accident. He retired due to a disability March 21, 1946, after a serious heart condition developed.

My dad, Robert Charles, followed his father, making the railroad his career.

I spent a lot of time in my grandfather's company after his retirement. Part of his ritual/therapy was a daily walk downtown to the depot with me in tow to see the passenger trains come in and confer with his mates. Since he had a lifetime pass, we also made periodic pilgrimages to various places along the line. I recall many a visit to the Pagoda in Reading where we had tea and fortune cookies before catching the next train back. On one occasion, we went as far as New Jersey where an old friend worked as projectionist in a movie theater. It was a thrill for a youngster to view a movie from the vantage point of the projection booth.

Later, my sister and I would accompany our parents to various rallies and entertainment programs the company sponsored for its employees and their families. As Christmas approached, mother again utilized those wonderful employee passes for a shopping trip to Philadelphia. I have no memory of specific gifts from those outings, but I do recall they always included a lunch at Bookbinder's, the oldest seafood restaurant in the city, now lamentably long gone.

This book is not about my family, though they are its inspiration. Nor is it meant to be a history of all the railroads that operated in the Anthracite Coal Region. My intent, rather, is to provide a glimpse of the life of some of the men who worked in the industry and their families, primarily in Northumberland and Schuylkill counties in the nineteenth and early twentieth centuries.

1

IN THE BEGINNING

"The Americans arrived but as of yesterday on the territory which they inhabit, and they have already changed the whole order of nature for their own advantage. They have joined the Hudson to the Mississippi and made the Atlantic Ocean communicate with the Gulf of Mexico, across a continent of more than five hundred leagues in extent which separates the two seas. The longest railroads that have been constructed up to the present time are in America."[1]

This comment by Alexis de Tocqueville, a French visitor to the United States early in the nineteenth century, illustrates how American entrepreneurs had taken advantage of a predominately-European innovation and begun utilizing it to make the nation an industrial giant.

Pennsylvania was at the forefront of that revolution.

Coal from Pennsylvania's anthracite region was first transported to market by wagon and on barges floated down the rivers. Since roads were not well-maintained and the rivers often froze in winter making transport difficult, the canal system, beginning in 1825 with completion of the Schuylkill Canal which extended from Pottsville to Philadelphia, a distance of more than a hundred miles, was seen as a great improvement. Two years after completion of the Erie Canal in New York, work commenced in 1827 on a canal from the Juniata River and along the west bank of the Susquehanna River to Northumberland, Northumberland County, and then on to Wilkes-Barre. A west branch of this

---

1. Democracy in America, Volume II. Alexis de Tocqueville.

canal continued north to Muncy and, eventually, a connection with the Erie Canal.

"What advantages has railroad over a canal for coal shipments?

"Besides that of quicker dispatch, railroads are advantageous in districts where canals, for want of water, would be impractical. This advantage is often felt in mining districts, and sometimes by the general trade, where it is necessary to cross dividing ridges at a level too high to obtain water for canal navigation."[2]

John Stevens (Courtesy of Encyclopedia Britannica.)

The railroad has its roots in Great Britain, where it was first utilized as a means of moving coal and farm goods to market.

Rails were utilized for the first time for moving freight in Pennsylvania in 1809 when Thomas Leiper connected quarries in Delaware County to a boat landing via a horse-drawn tramway.

But it was not a Pennsylvanian who brought the true railroad to the commonwealth. That honor goes to Colonel John Stevens of New Jersey. Stevens, an inventor who competed with Robert Fulton in the development of steam engines to move boats, is known as the father of American railroads.

Stevens was a pioneer in seeing the potential for passenger and freight transportation by railroad. He was granted the nation's first charter for a railroad company in 1815 by the New Jersey state legislature. This plan failed for lack of adequate funding, but Stevens didn't give up his dreams.

Ten years later he built and operated a prototype steam locomotive on his estate in Hoboken, N.J. A replica of the "John Stevens" is on display at the Railroad Museum of Pennsylvania at Strasberg, PA.

---

2. Fifth edition Coal Catechism, April 1906, Chapter 13.

*An early-model (probably 1880s) steam locomotive pulls into a depot.
(Courtesy of Larry Deklinski, Delado Photography; Northumberland County Historical
Society; and Paul Thomas Studios.)*

Stevens's sons Robert and Edwin started the Camden and Amboy, the first commercial railroad line in New Jersey.

With the rise of railroad fever, as its advantages began to be seen, Stevens was granted another charter by the Pennsylvania Legislature in 1823 for an eighty-mile line from Philadelphia to Columbia, Lancaster County. Again, plans faltered for lack of finances despite extensive promotion and a survey visit of the proposed route by Stevens.

Stevens died on March 6, 1838 before his dream of a railroad serving Pennsylvania could be achieved. But the spark had been lit.

The railroad came to Shamokin, my hometown, in 1838, an extension of the Danville & Pottsville Railroad from Sunbury and Paxinos. Cars were pulled by a wood-burning locomotive. Later this locomotive would make two daily trips, carrying coal to and returning with supplies for Shamokin. By 1853 the line had been extended to Mount Carmel.

Records show daily salaries of $2 for the engineer, $1.50 for the fireman, and $1 for the brakeman.

Sunbury RR station. (Courtesy of Larry Deklinski, Delado Photography; Northumberland County Historical Society; and Paul Thomas Studios.)

The Shamokin, Sunbury, and Lewisburg Railroad Company surveyed a route and constructed a line between Shamokin and Sunbury in 1883. In July of that year, the line was leased to the Philadelphia & Reading for 999 years.

THE PENNSY

There were prototypes and experiments at various levels, but it wasn't until April 13, 1846 that the scope of Stevens's dream was finally accomplished with the granting of a charter to the Pennsylvania Railroad.

There had been a Pennsylvania Railroad Company earlier, a state-owned and operated conglomerate of public works comprised of canals, short-line, and inclined plane railroads. But, faced with increasing competition from privately owned railroad companies in New York, New Jersey, and Maryland, the commonwealth saw advantage in granting charter to a privately-owned line in Pennsylvania.

A main objective of the new company was to link Philadelphia and Pittsburgh and thus gain access to the developing West. The Baltimore & Ohio already had plans in the works for a route from Baltimore to Pittsburgh, so it was

Crew of Engine No. 596 near Shamokin. Inset of Ed Lindermuth.
(Courtesy of Larry Deklinski, Delado Photography; Northumberland County Historical
Society; and Paul Thomas Studios.)

imperative for the Pennsy to move quickly to beat the B&O's goal of capturing this lucrative market.

John Edgar Thomson, a Quaker surveyor who had gained experience in Pennsylvania and other states, was enticed back to Pennsylvania and named chief engineer of the Pennsy. Under his guidance, the route was surveyed and contracts awarded to meet a legislative deadline.

Thomson achieved the goal, his efforts keeping the B&O out of Pittsburgh until 1871.

The 350-mile link was accomplished and trains began running between the two major Pennsylvania cities on February 15, 1854.

But Thomson didn't rest on his laurels. He plowed profits back into the company and bought or leased connecting lines extending into other states. Under his direction, the PRR would become the world's largest business enterprise and a model for technological and management innovation.

John Edgar Thomson

Horseshoe Curve vintage postcard.

Among the subsidiaries acquired by the Pennsy was the Northern Central Railway by which the Baltimore & Ohio had connected Baltimore and Sunbury, Pennsylvania, in its attempt to corner the northern markets. Completed in 1858, the line was acquired by the PRR in 1861. The NCR played an important role during the Civil War in troop and supply transport.

Let's now consider some of those technological innovations for which Thomson was responsible.

The first would be the Horseshoe Curve. The route laid out by Thomson followed the west bank of the Susquehanna River north to the confluence with the Juniata River at what would become Altoona. At this point it became necessary to ascend the heights of the Allegheny Mountains. Before the engineering miracle conceived by Thomson trains could only cross this barrier via the Allegheny Portage Railroad, which didn't operate at night.

The portage railroad—a technological leap in its own right—had been built in 1834 and utilized a combination of canals, horses, and steam locomotive to ascend the mountains. Using rope and specially-built cars, the engine hauled cars successively from one incline to another on tracks over the mountain on a 36-mile route.

Reading camelback locomotive at Shamokin. Top row, from left: Jim Madenford, in cab; Ed Lindermuth, author's great-uncle, and John Haas. Others not identified. (Courtesy of Larry Deklinski, Delado Photography; Northumberland County Historical Society; and Paul Thomas Studios.)

Thomson visualized another system, breaking down the grade for the ascent by a series of curves. The Horseshoe Curve is the largest of these.

This curve is 2,375 feet in length and 1,300 feet in diameter. For every 100 feet, the tracks bend nine degrees and 15 minutes, the entire curve totaling 220 degrees. The curve descends from an elevation of about 1,640 feet on the southern side to 1,600 feet on the northern flank.

And the entire thing was built by hand over a three-year period beginning in 1850 and achieving completion by the deadline of February 1854. Some four hundred laborers, primarily Irish immigrants, worked with picks and shovels for 12-hour days for an average pay of 25 cents an hour.

Completion of the curve reduced time for travel between Philadelphia and Pittsburgh from a week or more by wagon to approximately a day.

Another technological marvel which fell under Thomson's hand during the Philadelphia-Pittsburgh project was

Reading camelback locomotive No. 717 at Shamokin. Crew unidentified.
(Courtesy of Larry Deklinski, Delado Photography; Northumberland County Historical
Society; and Paul Thomas Studios.)

construction of one of three tunnels which bore through the
Allegheny Mountains.

The first tunnel had been bored in conjunction with the
commonwealth's portage railroad. It was purchased by the
PRR in 1857 and taken out of service until the 1890s when
it was expanded to two tracks and utilized for eastbound
traffic.

Under Thomson's direction, the "Summit" tunnel was
bored between 1851-54. This tunnel is 3,612 feet in length
at an elevation of 2,167 feet above sea level. After purchase
of the state's tunnel, the name "Allegheny" was appropriated
for Thomson's tunnel.

The *Sunbury American* reported on Feb. 4, 1854:

> The great tunnel of the Pennsylvania rail road through the
> Alleghany mountains has been completed, and a locomotive
> passed through it on Thursday, in about ten minutes time,
> moving at the rate of nearly six miles per hour. The cars
> will commence running regularly through the mountain on
> Monday, the 6th of February next.

Crew at new Reading engine house at Shamokin on May 1, 1931. Standing, from left, Harry Adams, carpenter; Harry Yocum, hostler's helper; George Wendell, hostler; Al Hummel, stationary boilerman; Milt Troutman, machinist; Clayton Deppen, storehouse; Harry Persing, blacksmith helper; Bill Esslick, boiler washer; Ben Wraggs, boilermaker, and John Murphy, machinist. Seated, from left, John Coleman, storekeeper; Bob Unger, airbrake inspector; Frank Klemick, fire cleaner; John Hower, blacksmith; Ellwood Spotts, boilermaker helper; Edward Yocum, laborer; Renold Perry, machinist; Frank Johns, boilermaker helper, and Robert Lindermuth, laborer, author's grandfather.
(Courtesy of Larry Deklinski, Delado Photography; Northumberland County Historical Society; and Paul Thomas Studios.)

A third tunnel, the Galitzin, was opened to the north of the Allegheny in 1904.

There would be other innovative directors in its future, but Thomson was responsible for the Pennsy's earliest success. Under his guidance it became the largest railroad in the world with 6,000 miles of tracks, remained solvent through a series of national panics that bankrupted many other enterprises and paid steady dividends to its investors.

The PRR played a strong role in the anthracite region and you'll be seeing the line mentioned more in future pages of this book.

THE READING COMPANY

The Reading, the line with which my family was most affiliated, was the successor of the Philadelphia and Reading

Reading Lines logo
(Courtesy of Reading Co.)

Reading Co. engine No. 462 at Shamokin, circa 1915. Crew unidentified. (Courtesy of Larry Deklinski, Delado Photography; Northumberland County Historical Society; and Paul Thomas Studios.)

Railway Company founded in 1833 and, thus, an older company than the Pennsy.

The P&R, along with the Little Schuylkill, a horse-drawn line, was one of the first railroads in the United States. Founded for the purpose of hauling coal from Pennsylvania's anthracite region to Philadelphia, it enjoyed almost immediate profitability.

Its 93-mile route from Pottsville, Schuylkill County, to Philadelphia had the distinction, upon completion in 1843, of being the first double track main line in the nation.

This route was laid out under the direction of Moncure Robinson, a Virginia native and self-taught surveyor/engineer who was early involved with canals and railroads, including the commonwealth's Allegheny Portage Railroad. He was hired as chief engineer by the newly chartered P&R and supervised construction of the line as well as the building of a distinctive stone bridge and a 1,932-foot long tunnel.

Despite stormy weather, which dropped four inches of snow along the route, the opening of the Pottsville railroad between that city and Philadelphia was marked with pomp and ceremony on Monday, Jan. 10, 1842.

A report in the Jan. 11 issue of the *Public Ledger,* Philadelphia, said 75 passenger cars carried 2,150 persons, including seven volunteer militia companies—three from

Pottsville, one from Schuylkill Haven, one from Warwicksburg (sic, I believe meant to be Orwigsburg) and another from Reading—and a number of bands providing music along the way, from the Schuylkill County community to the City of Brotherly Love.

"At Reading they were greeted with a salute of twenty-one guns from the Reading Artillerists, and at Norristown a similar compliment was paid them," the *Ledger* said.

Moncure Robinson (Courtesy of Wikipedia Commons)

"The cars carrying the immense number of passengers were drawn by a single engine, and, notwithstanding there was four inches fall of snow on the road at starting, performed its work admirably well, accomplishing the distance, ninety miles, in 6 1/2 hours running time.

"In the rear of the passengers there was a train of 52 burthen cars, loaded with 180 tons of coal, a part of which was mined the same morning four hundred and twelve feet below water level, and some few pieces of it brought to the Washington Hotel by the miners themselves for the inspection of the curious and doubting."

On arrival in the city, the military companies and bands marched through the principal streets to the applause of witnesses.

A delegation, including Mr. Robertson (newspaper spell—Robinson?), chief engineer; G. A. Nichols, superintendent; other officers of the railroad company and the Pottsville committee of arrangements were feted at the Washington Hotel.

On return to Pottsville that evening, a ball and other entertainments was planned.

Still, some journalists in Philadelphia weren't overly optimistic about the success of railroads, as may be seen in this May 31, 1842 dispatch in the *Public Ledger:*

Retirement of yardmaster Dawson Rahn (standing, right) at Shamokin 1954. Engineer Phil Haley in cab of diesel work train. Top row, from left, Sandy Kimmel, Gordon, conductor; Ernest Yeager, brakeman; Bob Nark, fireman; 'Porky' Kasker, Gordon; Bob Lindermuth, author's father, conductor, and 'Chubb' Kanaskie. Third row, standing from left, Joe Elliott, Clarence Murphy, Bob Bilder, Perry Getkins, Jim Smith. Second row, standing from left, John Ondush, clerk; Joe MacAlady, conductor; Harold Smith, agent; Cal Martz, yardmaster, and Rahn. Others not identified. (Courtesy Paul Thomas Studios)

The first train of fifty cars, containing 150 tons of coal, destined for Richmond on the Delaware, by the railroad, was loaded at Mr. Bast's mines on the West Branch Railroad. The train left Schuylkill Haven on Monday evening last, at four o'clock a.m., and was discharged in a vessel which set sail for an eastern port on the evening of the same day. This dispatch will give our readers some idea of the facility with which the coal business can be conducted as soon as the company have completed the necessary arrangements to accommodate those engaged in the trade. There is very little change in the trade in this region except that the demand has slackened off a little even at the low rates at which coal is disposed of. Per the last report 33,466 tons of coal were shipped from Schuylkill Haven for the week ending Thursday last. The

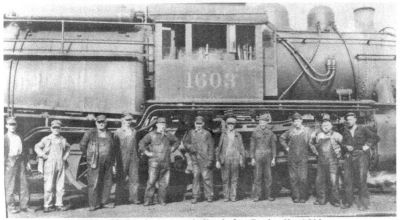

Unidentified train crew stainding before Engine No. 1603.
(Courtesy of Larry Deklinski, Delado Photography; Northumberland County Historical
Society; and Paul Thomas Studios.)

freight from Schuylkill Haven by canal is from five to ten cents per ton less than from Pottsville and Port Carbon.

Like those of the Pennsy, the first locomotives of the P&R were wood-burners. With its interests in anthracite, there was early intent to convert locomotives to the use of coal as fuel. This is made evident in the early minutes of management. A notation dated April 13, 1835 said, "Resolved that this board deem it of the utmost importance that the locomotive engines to be constructed for this Company be built with a view to the exclusive use of anthracite as fuel."

Early experiments were found wanting and the goal wasn't fully achieved until the mid 1850s.

In tandem with its early success, the P&R began buying up or leasing other short lines in surrounding areas of the state; built Port Richmond, then the largest railroad tidewater terminal in the world, from which coal could be loaded onto ships for export, and, most importantly, created the Philadelphia Coal and Iron Company, a subsidiary in 1871, which invested in the purchase of mines in the hard coal region. This would give the company a monopoly over coal from mining to marketing.

This move had a huge payout, making the Reading the largest company in the world with a gross value of $170 million in 1871 under the presidency of Franklin B. Gowen, a man we'll also hear more about in coming pages.

An editorial in the Saturday, Feb. 11, 1854 edition of the *Sunbury American* extolled the importance of coal to the nation's commerce. Though the editorial favored the prospect of the Susquehanna Railroad planned by the Baltimore & Ohio, it admitted Philadelphia's supremacy in the trade:

> This grand and imposing result has been attained by the construction of the Reading Railroad and the Schuylkill Canal—parallel improvements that penetrate the mines of Schuylkill.

The newspaper contended the natural destination of Schuylkill County's coal was Philadelphia and that of the Wyoming coal fields was the Great Lakes region and New York. But the editors saw Baltimore and the Southern Atlantic states as the natural destination of the coal of the Shamokin region.

Probably for this very reason, the Reading followed the example of the Pennsy and also began extending into other states as early as it did.

LAUDABLE STRATEGY

The *Evening Herald* of Shenandoah lauded the P&R on Saturday, Feb. 6, 1892 for what it called "the neatest piece of railroad strategy on record."

The *Herald* commented, "The acquisition of the Poughkeepsie bridge by the Philadelphia and Reading Company is a piece of masterly strategy. President McLeod has attained a position in the game which has been long and slowly played by competing railroads to gain control of this keystone of eastern traffic, which is almost impregnable.

"Practically speaking, Reading takes the place of the Delaware and New England Company, a corporation organized to own and operate a system of railways from New England to an undefined point at the southern extremity of Delaware."

IMPROVEMENTS

The *Shamokin Times* of Oct. 17, 1879 reported on some important improvements the Reading planned at Shamokin:

> The track through Cruikshank's Addition to the old Marshall breaker is to be extended, and a new track will be built along Shamokin Creek down to a point below the Liberty hose house, where a bridge will be constructed over Shamokin Creek and the new line will connect with the old track south of Independence street, at a point opposite the lockup.
>
> "As soon as this 'cut off' is completed all the freight and coal will pass over the new track, and the present track, from Liberty street to the round house at the east side of town, will be used only for passenger trains, and local freight to and from Shamokin. The freight and passenger depot will remain where it is now, at Rock street.

Early on, American railroads followed the precedent of the British and gave their locomotives names. The Reading was the first to break away from that practice. In 1871, they began replacing the names with numbers. The only exception to this rule was the naming of locomotives on the Reading's less extensive passenger service.

LEHIGH VALLEY RAILROAD

Another major line to be considered here is the Lehigh Valley, incorporated by the Pennsylvania Legislature on April 21, 1846. Six years later, thanks mainly to Asa Packer, one of Pennsylvania's more interesting entrepreneurs, construction began on a line connecting Easton and Mauch Chunk (now Jim Thorpe), where Packer resided.

A native of Connecticut, he is the epitome of the self-made man. As a teenager, he walked from his home

Asa Packer (Photo on display at Lehigh University and Packer House in Jim Thorpe (Mauch Chunk).

Lehigh Valley station at Centralia, Columbia County.
(Courtesy of Larry Deklinski, Delado Photography; Northumberland County Historical
Society; and Paul Thomas Studios.)

state to Pennsylvania in search of opportunity. Apprenticed as a carpenter, he soon found his niche building and repairing canal boats. In 1833, he settled at Mauch Chunk, acquired his own canal boat, carrying coal to Philadelphia and then set up a company to build boats and locks for the Lehigh Coal and Navigation Company, believed to be the first to ship coal to New York. Packer also invested in mining operations.

Already a wealthy man when the Lehigh was chartered, he saw advantage and went about acquiring most of the fledging company's stock and assumed the presidency of the railroad. He extended the main line into Luzerne and Schuylkill counties to directly connect with coal mines. By 1866, the railroad had extended to Mount Carmel in Northumberland County. Later, tracks would be laid into New York and New Jersey to connect with a wider market.

Packer also saw advantage in adding passenger trains, partially spurred by the beauty of Mauch Chunk and the Lehigh Gorge, already attracting visitors and earning the designation "The Switzerland of America." The *Shamokin Times* remarked in 1879 that many residents of that community were taking excursions to Mauch Chunk. Tourists were flocking to the Hotel Wahnetah at nearby Glen Onoko from New York and Philadelphia by the 1880s.

Mauch Chunk, circa 1864.
(Courtesy of Wikipedia Commons)

One of the popular tourist attractions was the Switch-back Railroad, a gravity fed line designed to haul coal from Summit Hill to the canal. Built in 1827 by the Lehigh Coal and Navigation Company and extended in the 1840s, it has the distinction of being the first railroad in Pennsylvania.

Packer founded Lehigh University, served in both the Pennsylvania and U.S. House, and was a democratic candidate for president in 1868. The mansion he built for himself is now another of the community's tourist attractions.

Packer has another interesting connection to this narrative. The Reading's first English-built locomotives were delivered by Packer's boats in 1838.

This from an article in the Feb. 5, 1892 *Evening Herald*, Shenandoah:

Yesterday morning passenger train No. 18, of the Lehigh Valley Railroad, left Black Creek 15 minutes late, made four stops, and made the run to Delano, a distance of 18 miles, in 21 minutes, reaching there on time. The run appears more extraordinary when it is considered that the road from Black Creek to Delano is all upgrade. The train consisted of the engine and two cars. The engine is numbered 612 and was recently turned out of the shops at Hazleton.

"The crew consisted of Charles Price, engineer; Hiram Henry, fireman; Jacob Wanamaker, conductor; Philip Adams, baggagemaster; Henry Crilly, brakeman.

DELAWARE, LACKAWANNA & WESTERN

This line, which had its roots in the Scranton, Lackawanna County area, played a lesser role in my area of Pennsylvania but is still worthy of mention.

Incorporated in 1853, it was like the others we've mentioned the result of consolidation of a variety of lines stretching back to the Liggett's Gap Railroad which ran track from Scranton to Great Bend, just below the New York border.

Between the time of its founding and the mid-1870s, through more mergers and buyouts, it had stretched its tentacles deep into New York and New Jersey.

One of those branches stretched into Northumberland County and connected with the Pennsy. When abandoned by Conrail in 1984, it became the North Shore short line, which continues to operate.

The Lackawanna's most profitable cargo was anthracite coal, though it also transported other vital commodities and carried city-weary vacationers to the Poconos on its passenger branch.

Like the others, the decline of coal as fuel, competition from trucking, and other economic factors hastened its demise.

STANDARD GAUGE

At the beginning, railroads determined their own track gauges and there were considerable variances between them. It wasn't until the various lines began connecting with one another that the need for standardization became apparent.

The early use of British-built locomotives by the bigger companies did result in adoption of a standard gauge, though it was not adopted by all.

This dispute over gauge actually resulted in a conflict known as the Erie Railroad War, in which "special constables" sworn in by Erie's Mayor Alfred King began ripping up tracks of railroad companies which didn't adhere to the city's adopted six-foot gauge (1,829 mm) in December 1853. The result was fisticuffs and even the firing of pistol shots

Baldwin Locomotive Works (Horace L. Arnold, 1894).

(fortunately no deaths resulted). It took action by the Pennsylvania Legislature in January 1854 to settle the matter.

It wasn't until June 1886 that all major railroads in the United States adopted a standard gauge of approximately 4-foot, 9-inches (1,448 mm).

LOCOMOTIVE BUILDERS

Matthias Baldwin, a Philadelphia tinkerer and inventor, was the primary builder of steam locomotives for all of Pennsylvania's railroad companies.

After a career as a jeweler and builder of a variety of mechanical devices, he was asked by Peale's Philadelphia Museum to build a miniature working locomotive for an exhibition in 1831. This led to an order for a full-size locomotive to be used by a short-line in the Philadelphia area.

"Old Ironsides" went into service on Nov. 23, 1832 for the

Drawing of Baldwin from the National Cyclopedia of Biography, Vol. 9, 1899.

Broad Street station before 1911. (Courtesy of Wikipedia Commons.)

Philadelphia, Germantown, and Norristown Railroad and remained in use for 20 years. This little prototype had an initial speed of one-mile-per hour, the speed increased to 28 miles per hour by later refinements.

Despite economic difficulties during the Panic of 1837, Baldwin persevered and by 1840, his fledgling company, originally located on North Broad street, had turned out 150 locomotives. By the mid-1880s, the company Baldwin founded had become the nation's largest manufacturer of steam locomotives and was shipping its product around the world.

Reading constructed the largest shops in the nation in the first few years of the twentieth century in its namesake community, enabling the company to build some of its own engines. But the majority of its fleet was acquired from Baldwin.

The Pennsy also built some locomotives in its Altoona shops. Like the Reading, its primary outsource was Baldwin.

Baldwin's principal competitors were the Lima Locomotive Works of Lima, Ohio, and the American Locomotive Company of Schenectady, New York. Lima, founded in 1878, merged with Baldwin in 1951. ALCO, founded in 1901

Pennsy Altoona Works. (Courtesy of Pennsylvania Railroad Collection.)

through merger with a number of smaller manufacturers, terminated locomotive production in 1969.

Baldwin failed to see the future in diesel production and maintained emphasis on building steam locomotives and gradually lost its preeminence in the market. Baldwin-Lima shut down in 1972.

Baldwin locomotives are included in the collection at the Steamtown National Historical Site in Scranton, and at the Railroad Museum of Pennsylvania, Strasburg, Lancaster County.

HISTORIC ENGINE

The Catawissa, an engine used on the first trip by railroad between Tamaqua and Port Clinton, Schuylkill County, in 1843, was exhibited at the St. Louis Exposition in 1904.

A Mr. Bensinger, formerly of Mahanoy City, told the *Danville Intelligencer* of July 29, 1904 that he was 11 years old when he witnessed the start of the 20-mile run.

"The road was fitted up with wooden rails on top of which was scrap iron. The new 'invention' created all sorts of excitement throughout that region, people really fearing it as the forerunner of the end of the world. This twenty miles of roads was not originally intended for passenger traffic, but for the carrying of coal. It pulled what were then called drift cars and was able to pull about twenty of them at one time.

"Each car carried about one and a half tons of coal, or 3,000 pounds, while now any ordinary railroad engine hauls a train of twenty or more cars, each one of which carries from twenty to thirty tons of the black diamonds.

"This improvement and forward step shows that either the minister of seventy years ago was wrong when he said that it was the devil's work, or the old fellow must have been getting in his work pretty lively ever since."

2

RAILROAD TOWNS

TOWN BUILDERS

Unlike the coal barons, the rail magnates in the eastern United States weren't big on town building, a practice which became more common as the nation and the railroads expanded into the western states.

While the Pennsylvania coal operators had found it both convenient and profitable to set up company towns or "patches" where their employees could live, the railroad companies seemed content to let their workers find their own living quarters. Single men often found lodging in boarding houses while the married rented, unless they were fortunate enough to be an engineer or conductor earning more than the average crewman and, thus, able to buy a house in the town from which they worked.

Towns grew up along the lines because of the convenience a railroad provided in moving goods to market. But there are few towns in Pennsylvania actually created by the rail lines. The best known of those that were created by the railroads would be Altoona in Blair County, Renova in Clinton County, and Sayre in Bradford County.

ALTOONA

The town of Altoona was founded by the PRR in 1849 as the site for a shop and maintenance facility, which at one time was the largest in the world. The original facility included machine, woodworking, and blacksmith shops, a locomotive repair shop, and a foundry.

Philadelphia & Reading station, Shamokin. (Courtesy of Larry Deklinski, Delado Photography; Northumberland County Historical Society; and Paul Thomas Studios.)

The town was incorporated as a borough on Feb. 6, 1854. John A. Wright laid out the building lots after his father Archibald, representing the railroad, purchased the farm of David Robeson, a 224-acre tract. The younger Wright conveyed the deed for the property to the railroad in 1851.

Coal, iron, and lumber necessary for the railroad's purpose were all available in the vicinity. Within a year the shop was engaged in repairing railway cars and making parts for locomotives, bridge parts, and wrought iron rail tracks.

Population of the new town rose from about 2,000 in 1854 (more than 1,000 employed in the shops) to more than 10,000 in the next decade. Growth was further stimulated by the demand for locomotives and troop transport during the Civil War.

There's controversy about the origin of the town's name. Some connect it to the Latin word *Altus*, meaning "high" and reflecting its mountainous surroundings, while others claim a Native American derivation traced to Wright. A more likely origin is that attributed to Colonel Beverly Mayer, the engineer who laid out the tracks in the town, who is said to have named the town for the German city of Altona, which also has links to railroading.

Altoona remains a railroad city, though its economy is no longer solely committed to that industry.

RENOVA

Renova was also created in 1863 as a site for a repair shop with the ulterior purpose of stifling competition from other railroads on the route to Lake Erie.

Much smaller than Altoona, Renova is nestled in the Clinton County mountains along the West Branch of the Susquehanna River. The town was originally built by the Philadelphia & Erie Railroad, one of those smaller lines eventually bought up by the Pennsylvania Railroad.

The *Northumberland County Democrat* reported on Thursday, Nov. 17, 1898:

> Ten of the employees of the blacksmith shops at Renova have been transferred to Erie for the purpose of assisting on extra car work. There is an extra rush of work at Erie and there is totally inadequate manpower to get the repair completed. For that reason it was found necessary to ask assistance from the Renova shops.

Even before the railroads provided easy access, the Renova area was a popular resort destination because of its clean mountain air and opportunity for outdoor activities, particularly hunting, fishing, and hiking.

At its high point, the town had a population of around 5,000 people, the railroad and its shops being the major employer. By 2010, the census shows a drop in population to slightly more than 1,000 people but the area's popularly as an outdoors activity magnet hasn't declined and the town's Flaming Foliage Festival in October remains a major tourist attraction.

SAYRE

Sayre, the largest borough in Bradford County, owes its existence to Asa Packer.

In the summer of 1870, Howard Elmer, a banker, and his partners Charles Anthony and James Fritcher, bought up a tract of land known as the Pine Plains between the towns of Waverly and Athens. At Elmer's urging, Packer decided to locate a railroad repair facility on the tract for his Lehigh Valley Railroad. At the time, the Lehigh was making a pitch to connect with the Erie Railroad at Waverly. The deal was completed with the assistance of Robert Heysham Sayre, chief engineer of the Lehigh who had responsibility for the railroad's extension northward in Pennsylvania and New York.

Sayre was incorporated on January 27, 1891 and named for the Lehigh's chief engineer.

For a time, the Lehigh's main shop building at Sayre was considered the largest structure of its kind under one roof.

Sayre never lived in the town named for him, but Packer's son Robert did, moving to the community after being appointed superintendent with responsibility for the Lehigh's northern operations. The Robert Packer Hospital in Sayre was named after him.

Sayre is the subject of a legend not founded in fact but popularized by a number of writers including Brad Steiger. In the 1880s, Dr. G. P. Donehoo, then state historian, and associates A. B. Skinner and W. K. Moorehead, excavated a burial mound. Later, rumors spread that they'd discovered skeletons of giants with horned skulls.

The official reports of Donehoo and the others reveal nothing to substantiate the claims, though the legends persist in surfacing now and again.[1]

The 2010 census shows Sayre with a population of 5,587 persons.

Though not created by the railroads, many others became known as "railroad towns" because of the importance of the industry to their welfare or due to the number of railroad families who resided in the community. One such example is New Ringgold in Schuylkill County, which was

---

1. Donehoo, George P. (1918). "The Susquehanna Archaeological Expedition." *The Second Report of the Historical Commission of Pennsylvania.* Pennsylvania Historical Commission: 126–151.

extolled as such in an article in the Wednesday, May 27, 1891 issue of the *Evening Herald*, Shenandoah.

"New Ringgold is not only one of the prettiest, but is also one of the most enterprising little towns of Schuylkill County," the *Herald* said. "It is a railroaders' town and many of the 'Knights of the Road' have their homes there.

"It is not a business centre, the people mainly depending upon farming as a means of support, and it has two stores, one shoemaker's shop, one blacksmith shop and two hotels; but the basis of its claim to enterprise is a shoe factory, which gives employment to a number of hands and is doing a good business."

The *Herald* described New Ringgold's P&R depot as an "object of admiration." The depot was in charge of John F. Reeser, a Tamaqua native who began his career with the Little Schuylkill Navigation Company. Reeser was a member of Camp 100, Sons of America (also known as the Round-heads), one of the many fraternal organizations in existence at the time.

Another article in the same issue of the *Herald* on the development of the nearby Lakeside resort also commented on the value of the railroads to Schuylkill County.

"When the project of running the Pennsylvania railroad into Schuylkill County was stamped as ridiculous on the ground that two companies could not make profits out of a divided tonnage, he maintained a view to the contrary, very wisely, too, as shown by developments of to-day.

Lakeside Park, Pa.

Lakeside Park vintage postcard.

"When the Reading railroad was first projected, said he, there were not more than 4,000 people in the county. The population is now nearly 160,000. In twenty years from now the county will have double that number of people and the two railroads passing through the Schuylkill Valley will have more than they can do.

"The development of its resources have hardly been commenced. Property will greatly enhance in value and the valley will be a hive of industry. There is an enormous quantity of coal, iron, limestone, etc., to be developed."

3

DAILY LIFE

Aside from his employment, the daily life of a railroader was little different from that of his neighbors with other jobs. In the nineteenth century, a householder in his off-hours still had an assortment of chores that needed tending. There might be wood to be cut and stored or coal spilled from passing freights to be picked and carted home for the stoves, there might be a cow to be milked or chickens to be fed, possibly a horse to be tended and the necessary work to maintain a house and yard. If he was away from home on the job, some of these chores could fall on the wife and older children. If not, they'd await his return home.

I mentioned in the preceding paragraph the common custom of picking coal lost from passing freights. It was generally an acceptable and tolerated practice. There were, however, times when it could be dangerous—most commonly when the picker failed to see or hear an approaching train and didn't get off the tracks in time. A Shamokin man had a frightening experience of another kind in 1876, which was reported in the Jan. 27 *Shamokin Herald*.

William Dilliplain, 23, who lived with his widowed mother at Franklin and Spurzheim streets was picking coal on a dirt bank near the Daniel Webster colliery when he heard a shot and a bullet whizzed by his head.

"Hastily turning about he discovered a man in the bush at the foot of the hill, who just then fired another shot, the ball cutting Dilliplain's hat rim and grazing his forehead, drawing blood."

The frightened young man abandoned his task and raced home.

The newspaper described him as a quiet, inoffensive citizen and concluded, "It is supposed the party who did the shooting mistook him for someone else."

When time wasn't engaged with these necessary tasks, the railroader would most likely seek diversion and entertainment. These varied with the season and available cash. Some, unfortunately, fell victim to gambling and drinking, vices all too common to the miners and other workmen in the coal region. Others, along with their families, sought relief from labor in a variety of ways described in contemporary newspapers. Some of these, as well as other events impacting their lives, follow:

REVIVALS

Religious revival services drew large attendance throughout the country, and none were larger than those conducted by Evangelists Dwight L. Moody and Ira D. Sankey.

The Sunbury American of January 28, 1876 reported the pair had just completed services in Philadelphia and raised $100,000 in collections which were being donated to the Young Men's Christian Association for a new building being constructed for the nation's centennial celebration.

"The expenses of the revival services, amounting to nearly thirty thousand dollars, were all met by voluntary contributions. One mother moved to gratitude for the happy conversion of a son through the labors of the Evangelists, gave a diamond ring as a thank offering. This ring, enriched by the circumstances we relate, was instantly purchased by a gentleman for one thousand dollars."

POPULAR ENTERTAINMENT

Concerts and other musical events were a prominent source of entertainment for our ancestors throughout the coal region.

Excelsior station. (Courtesy of Larry Deklinski, Delado Photography; Northumberland County Historical Society; and Paul Thomas Studios.)

The *Shamokin Herald* reported in its Thursday, July 27, 1882 issue that the Excelsior Cornet Band held a fundraising picnic on the preceding Saturday, July 22, which the newspaper described as a " . . . complete success and enjoyable affair."

The newspaper said the event raised between $150 and $175 for the community-based band and the organization was looking forward to holding more such events.

"The grove in which the event was held is opposite the P&R railroad depot and convenient also to the Lehigh Valley Railroad. This was the first time a picnic was held in this grove and officials plan to make improvements for future events. In the refreshment line, demand exceeded supply. The boys had laid in a good supply but could have sold nearly double the amount."

The *Herald* reported more than a hundred people from Shamokin attended the picnic. "The Trevorton Band was in attendance all day. They retired in the evening before the 'machine' was put into 'full blast' and consequently missed the most enjoyable part of the programme." The St. Edward's, Kosciusko and Citizens bands of Shamokin played for the evening and the *Herald* noted, "The music was plenty and good."

"A platform was erected and all desiring to trip the 'light fantastic' had the pleasure of doing so to the music of the orchestras in attendance."

The only blot on the event appears to have been a dispute between two parties from Shamokin which ended with one participant receiving a cut on the face, though the *Herald* said the unpleasantness "was settled at the depot before boarding the train back home."

FIRE COMPANIES

Volunteer fire companies are still the norm in the coal region where communities seldom have the financial resources to pay for these necessary emergency services. Many railroad workers were active volunteers, including my grandfather, his brother Edward, and my dad, all active members of the Independence. Apparently not all members of the community were as dedicated, as may be seen from this article in the Oct. 3, 1879 issue of the *Shamokin Times*:

It is time that our citizens should wake up to the importance of helping our hose companies if the firemen are to remain in service. The hose companies have been struggling along, trying to keep up their organizations, but some of them are in debt and unless relief is given they must go out of service and allow their property to be sold.

"The Liberty, we understand, will not be able to take their carriage out any more until some of their liabilities are met, and they are expecting notice almost any day that their property will be sold. The Independence Fire Association held a festival last week to raise means, but the festival was so poorly patronized that the boys were greatly discouraged. The Rescue

Ed Lindermuth family photo. (Courtesy of Larry Deklinski, Delado Photography; Northumberland County Historical Society; and Paul Thomas Studios.)

Independence Fire Co. (Courtesy of Larry Deklinski, Delado Photography; Northumberland County Historical Society; and Paul Thomas Studios.)

and Friendship companies also have expenses to meet and they should not be expected to run to fires and receive nothing in return. The hook and ladder company is the only one that is serene and happy.

"Why cannot some united effort be made to help the hose companies? We would suggest, as a starter, that a grand union fair or festival be gotten up, the proceeds to be divided between the several fire companies.

LIKE BROTHERS

Railroaders were a close-knit fraternity. They had a bond similar to that of soldiers, understandable between men whose lives often depended on that of their brothers.

An example of this friendship may be seen in a gathering held in the dispatcher's office of the Northern Central in Shamokin and reported in the March 4, 1882 *Shamokin Times*. Daniel Boughner, a distant cousin on my mother's side and a passenger conductor, who was leaving for Nebraska, was feted in a surprise gathering.

"Mr. Boughner was given to understand that the Superintendent desired to see him at the office on important railroad business, and Daniel was ushered into the presence of some twenty of his friends."

One of his friends, W. B. Bird, gave a speech, saying, "We are come together to honor a fellow railroader—to extend some fitting tribute of our respect and esteem to one who after seventeen years of faithful service on this division among us, is about to leave to seek a fortune in the great west as a tiller of the soil."

As a token of their esteem, the railroaders presented Boughner with a Remington breech-loader rifle and a hundred rounds of ammunition.

THE NATIONAL SPORT

Baseball has always been a favorite sport in the coal region, which produced some stellar players over the years. But winning a game was not the main objective of a 'famous game' played at Schuylkill Haven, according to a story in the Sept. 17, 1887 issue of the *Pottsville Republican.*

"The respective nines were under principal rule to be observed was that no man should have a glass of beer until he reached third base. It is unnecessary to say that not one member of the nines failed to reach the beer and it is equally remarkable that not one reached the home base. The fight for the championship that followed the game is not fully reported, but it is said the score was at least two or three runs."

A more serious outlook was expected when a Shamokin team requested games with the Old Timers of Danville in 1904. The *Danville Intelligencer* of June 17 said Shamokin sought two games on July 4.

"Shamokin wants a good drawing card for that day and the fact that it is considering the Old Timers indicates the high esteem in which the Danville veterans are held in neighboring towns and can be viewed in no other light than a compliment."

The Old Timers were also to be an attraction for the opening of the (Edgewood?) "park" at Shamokin on June 25.

"Shamokin and Danville are old time base ball rivals and a red hot game is expected when the two teams cross bats on the 25th," the newspaper said. "Shamokin seemed to have a shade of the best of it with Danville during the last season, but whether that team will be able to hold its prestige in face of the fight that the Old Timers will put up is an element of doubt which is going to make the next game real interesting."

BIG PRIZES

Talk about truth in advertising. Few companies these days might be expected to follow the example of the New England Tea Company of Boston when the firm opened a new store in 1887 in Shamokin. A railroader was among the beneficiaries.

The *Shamokin Herald,* on Friday, Nov. 4, 1887, reported on the unusual advertising scheme.

In order to introduce goods when the store opened at 22 Shamokin St., souvenirs were placed in each can of tea or coffee sold for a limited period of time. These souvenirs included gold, silver and nickel watches, genuine diamond, ruby, sapphire, pearl, emerald, turquoise and amethyst jewelry and various other gifts of lesser value.

The company gave assurance each can sold during this introductory period would include a souvenir. The one and a half pound cans of tea or coffee sold for a dollar each.

"This expensive and novel way of advertising will be discontinued in a few days," the *Herald* reported. "when these really choice goods will be sold strictly on their merits, at the same price, same quality, and quantity, but without the souvenir. The tea and coffee alone without any regard to the souvenir are worth more than the price asked."

As proof the offer was genuine, the *Herald* appended a lengthy list of patrons who had already found such souvenirs in their coffee and tea cans.

The entire list is too long to include here, but some of the winners were:

T. R. Hayes, 11 Spruce St., diamond ring; Mrs. Catherine Conrad, Franklin street, silver cup; W. G. Wheaton, a railroad engineer, $20 gold piece; Joseph Berner, Excelsior, silver pickle caster and a gold ring; Miss Annie Simmonds, dining room girl, National Hotel, diamond ring; Mrs. Hannah Bowler of Sunbury, ladies gold watch; Walter Shelinsky, a miner of Franklin street, diamond ring; Sylvester Shekowskie, Excelsior, stem winding watch; Mrs. Jennie Noll, Commerce street, silver cup; Mrs. Marie E. Gutshall, Gosstown, ladies solid gold band ring, and Miss Carrie Graham, dressmaker, a pair of genuine diamond ear drops.

NELLIE BURKE

The Shamokin area was in a state of excitement in the fall of 1890 for the opening of the second annual agricultural fair.

An article in the Sept. 26 edition of the *Shamokin Herald* said a large crowd was already on hand and the railroad companies were running special passenger trains down to Weigh Scales for horse races, exhibitions, and other planned events.

"The town is filled with strangers today. They hold down the street corners, do these sharp looking fakirs, and sporting men with an eye for a fast horse. Then there are petite blondes, gushing brunettes, and rosy maidens whose sun kissed cheeks declare their residence among the green pastures and golden grain fields."

A popular attraction between races was the Nellie Burke Hippodrome which would offer exhibitions of "horsemanship, chariot racing, trained riderless horses and greyhounds."

Nellie Burke, a native of Omaha, Nebraska, first won her reputation in the West for long distance racing, defeating competitors in races of 20 to a hundred miles. Later she became enamored of the track, competing around the country and providing exhibitions with her horses and a pack of greyhounds. A famous feature of her exhibition was driving four horses abreast in a Roman chariot.

The *Herald* described her as ". . . a pleasant little woman, rather stout and with more information lurking in her head about horses than can be found out in seven counties. She is thoroughly conversant with business matters, and the person that gets the better of her will have to get up before daybreak."

The scheduled trotter races attracted competitors from as far away as New York and Virginia, though a number were from the area. These included Thomas L. McNamara, Paxinos; F. D. Raker, Shamokin; W. W. Weidensaul, Mount Carmel; L. P. Holliday, Shamokin; F. M. Dogget, Shamokin; John McLane, Shamokin, and H. W. Becker, Girardville.

Apparently, horses weren't the only thing being wagered upon. The newspaper warned readers to be aware of ". . . the polished thimble rigger, the monte man and the champions of the sweat board."

ATLANTIC CITY

Atlantic City was a popular destination for Anthracite Coal Region residents long before the advent of casinos.

This was stressed in an article in the March 7, 1890 issue of the *Sunbury Weekly*, commenting on the Reading Company's new depot and an expected greater volume of travel with the opening of the spring season.

"Those of our readers who know Atlantic City only as a hot weather resort would be amazed to witness the evidence of life and activity now observable there. The largest of all our coast resorts, it well deserves its title of The American Brighton, having within the past few years been metamorphosed from a mere summer pleasuring place to a great and permanent sanitarium and abode of recreation.

"The spring season is now booming; all the leading hotels are open, and during the daily promenade hour the beach is crowded with votaries of fashion and seekers after health and rest."

Encouraged by the growth of travel to the resort, the Reading had built a new depot, reputed to be the "finest and most complete railway structure on the coast." The depot was 550 feet in length and had a frontage of 300 feet on Atlantic Avenue, the main thoroughfare.

"The train sheds are 450 feet long, with room for six tracks, and between these are platforms twenty-five feet wide. The capacious waiting rooms are artistically finished in oak with mahogany furnishings and rich curtains.

"Architecturally, the station is a beauty, and its great dimensions will enable railroad people to handle immense crowds without difficulty or delay. Arrangements have been made to augment the motive power and car equipment to meet the expected 'boom,' and Reading officials predict a phenomenally big season of travel."

THE LIMITED

An article in the *Sunbury American* on Feb. 14, 1890 extolled the virtue of the Pennsylvania Limited, a passenger train service between New York City and Chicago.

The Limited was launched on June 15, 1887 and continued until 1902 when it was replaced by the Pennsylvania Special. The Limited, which made stops in both Shamokin and Sunbury, was the first to include the vestibule, an enclosed platform at the end of each car which allowed protected access to the entire train.

The *American* noted that the Limited offered several services unique in the history of passenger travel.

"As it speeds across the continent there are flashed over the wires, to meet or overtake it, the fluctuations of the New York and Philadelphia stock markets, and there are also posted on its bulletins full reports of the doings in the foreign and domestic financial markets. Thus the wayfaring man reads as he runs.

"In order that the traveler may dispatch any commission which these reports may suggest, or dispose of any current correspondence, a stenographer and typewriter is provided for the free use of the train's patrons. He will take the dictation of letters or telegrams, and see that they are forwarded from the train. Thus may business proceed though the counting room be many miles away."

Pennsylvania Limited. (Courtesy of Pennsylvania Railroad Collection.)

Nor were the needs of women forgotten.

"For their convenience, a waiting maid is assigned to each train, whose duty is to serve as ladies maid in all that the term implies. Ladies without escort, ladies with children, and invalids are the particular objects of their care. So that one's own maid may be left at home, and yet the fair traveler may receive assistance of one well trained in the duties of her vocation."

Other features mentioned in the article were the observation car, superior sleeping apartments, bathrooms for both sexes, a dining car "unexcelled in service and cuisine," smoking and reading apartments, and a barber saloon.

BENEFICIAL IMPROVEMENTS

The *Evening Herald* of Shenandoah gloated in its July 13, 1891 issue as railroad officials confirmed a rumor the newspaper had reported the previous week about transportation improvements beneficial to the area.

The *Herald* said the Philadelphia and Reading Railroad Company had announced plans to build a short line parallel with the Pennsylvania Railroad to Gilberton from Frackville and to Shenandoah. "The company has been holding back long enough to see the advantage of a line such as the Pennsy controls from this town to Frackville."

The newspaper speculated that as soon as the P&R completed this new line all its passenger traffic from Ashland, Girardville, Mahanoy Plane, Shenandoah, and Mahanoy City to Pottsville would be sent from Frackville.

"Lakeside is soon to become a booming place. All traffic from Hazleton to Tamaqua and Philadelphia on the new Hazleton branch of the P&R will pass through that place."

It was also anticipated that the Pennsy would be laying a line of its own from Frackville to Wetherill Junction.

"This activity in railroad circles carries with it indications that should greatly encourage our people. It means new outlets for the coal and a general activity that must revert to the benefit of the people of Shenandoah and other towns north-of-the-mountain. It means that good times are ahead and, with patience, the people may yet be able to regain what they have lost for so many months."

In addition to this good news, the *Herald* reported all the collieries in the district were working steady and, for the first time in years, there was a scarcity of labor.

NEW AND NEAT

That was the headline on this Feb.2, 1892 report by the *Evening Herald*:

John W. Weeks, who purchased Jones' saloon and restaurant, at 17 South Main street, has had the place so extensively altered and improved as to make it almost new. He has put in an entire new stock of ales, porters, beers, segars, etc., and has annexed to the place an excellent eating department, which will be under the direction of 'Felt' Beyrant, the well known caterer of town. With the alterations he has made and the acquisition of Mr. Beyrant, Mr. Weeks can now pride himself of having one of the best restaurants in the region.

NO FUTURE FOR COAL

Imagine the despair of miners, railroaders and others whose livelihood was dependent on the industry when they read in the Feb. 4, 1892 issue of the *Evening Herald* that coal's days were numbered?

"The Electrical Progress is authority for the statement that the time is near-by when the stores, dwelling houses and offices, and the modes of travel, whether by land or sea, will be heated by electricity.

"The architect of the future will plan his house or business apartments to provide for the electric heater in place of the dirt, dust, soot and ash contrivance of the present day; the heat developed by the coal that has heretofore been carted into our cellars will be brought into the house on cleanly (interior conduit) wires and distributed throughout the house so carefully and practically as scarcely to be observable, and when the temperature of the room is too low, the occupant will simply press a button or turn a switch and, presto change, the room gradually assumes the proper temperature, and the heat is recognized, but the source is unseen."

The writer went on to explain how in hot weather comfort could be assured with the touch of another button, starting an electric fan. He also stressed that theaters, concert halls, railway cars, and ocean steamers would all be heated by electricity.

"In general use, consider the safety and neatness and also the immense labor-saving qualities of the electric heater, removes the unsightliness and disagreeable odor of the burning, dirty, dusty coal.

"There is no reason to doubt that by the time electric heating is as well developed as that of electric lighting and power, that generating stations will be established throughout the United States for that particular purpose."

FAIR FUN

What county fairs, such as that at Bloomsburg, have become to more recent generations, the Shamokin Agricultural and

Driving Park Association Fair was to our ancestors, including railroader families.

This is demonstrated by an article in the Sept. 16, 1892 edition of the *Shamokin Herald* announcing the grand opening of the event on the following Tuesday. It was reported preparations for the four-day fair had been under way for the past three months.

> As in former years the merry fakirs will be present with seductive games and cheery voices beguiling the innocent into making money easily. The merry-go-rounds, peanut stands, lunch counters, lemonade joints, cough drop man, side shows, cane stands and weight machine will be seen, and if the weather is chilly enough, the dashing sport with light overcoat and magnetic eye will fluctuate from place to place playing the games, taking in heat and exchanging covert glances with rosy cheeked damsels clad in blue flannel, jaunty sailor hat and tan colored shoes. The band will play inspiring airs, hand organs will yield forth 'Mery Green,' 'Ta-ra-ra,' etc., clowns will climb slippery poles and sprinters will try to circle the track in Nancy Hank time.

It was anticipated farmers and their families would flock from near and far for the attractions.

The writer derided 'dead beats' who would ". . . occupy hill sides and treetops, taking everything in for nothing, or rather, trying to, as the view is rather indistinct, owing to the great distance from the outside to the grand stand and points of enjoyment generally."

Excursion trains were expected to run hourly on both the Central and Reading railroads.

Richard Hugo's circus was to offer performances daily in front of the grand stand and a major attraction was the horse races which would be held in various classes on all four days of the fair.

BODY-SNATCHERS

A bizarre attempt at body snatching in Sunbury, Northumberland County, was accidentally thwarted by a railroad brakeman, it was reported in the Friday, Aug. 14, 1891 edition of the *Shamokin Herald*.

Soon after the death in 1886 of John B. Packer, prominent lawyer, businessman and former state representative, guards had been placed around his grave in response to rumors an attempt would be made to remove his remains and hold them for ransom. As time passed and no such attempt occurred, the family elected to remove the guards on Aug. 1, 1891.

The *Herald* reported the brakeman, identified only as Meyers, was walking down the railroad tracks early on the morning of Aug. 13 he heard a noise in the cemetery, which was opposite the lower yard of the Pennsylvania Railroad. "Listening intently for a minute, he imagined he heard the rattle of dirt and ringing of picks. He was startled for a while, then he arrived at the conclusion that the sexton, in order to escape the heat of the mid-day to prepare a grave for somebody, had chosen the cool hours of early morn to do his work.

"Not quite satisfied, Meyers leaped over the fence and proceeded in the direction of the noise. It was dark and in walking by a grave, fifty feet from the sound, Meyers tripped and fell over a tombstone. The fall produced considerable noise and when he arose Meyers was frightened to see three men run rapidly past him and into the underbrush.

"The brakeman ran back to the railroad and securing companions once more invaded the graveyard and found a number of picks and shovels over the grave of Mr. Packer. The mound had entirely disappeared and almost a foot of earth excavated from the surface. No trace of the would-be body snatchers could be found. Meyers was rewarded with a fair purse for his timely discovery."

UNHINGED HIS MIND

Catarrh is a medical condition in which the nose and other air passages become filled with mucus. Usually associated with a cold or flu, it may be uncomfortable but is not generally considered of serious consequence.

But in an article in the Friday, June 12, 1891 edition of the *Shamokin Herald,* catarrh was blamed for having unbalanced the mind of a passenger train engineer and, possibly, putting fellow crewmen and passengers at risk.

The incident occurred the previous day when Buck Elder, identified as a brother-in-law of Frank Brindle of Shamokin, was engineer on a Pennsylvania Railroad Company passenger train bound from Pottsville to Wilkes-Barre.

After running a short distance from Pottsville, the *Herald* reported, Elder suddenly halted the train and asked his conductor Zach Moyer, another former Shamokin man, for instructions. Moyer thought the engineer was joking and told him to proceed.

"All right, Zach," the engineer responded. "If you say so."

"The train rushed on for a while and them came to another quick stop. This time Elder wanted the tank filled, despite the fact that plenty of water was aboard. After two more runs and requests from Elder for more water and orders, the conductor got on the engine and by continuous talk and strategic moves managed to have the train continue the run to Wilkes-Barre."

That evening, after the incident was reported to the company, Elder was laid off and brought to Sunbury by his wife. There the man's odd actions were attributed to catarrh and plans were made to take him to Philadelphia for treatment.

BACK FROM THE DEAD

How would you react if a spouse you thought long dead suddenly turned up at your front door?

That was the situation faced by a Shamokin woman as reported in the Friday, June 19, 1891 issue of the *Shamokin Herald*. According to the report, Mrs. William Madden, who operated a boarding house at Rock and Water streets, was preparing supper for boarders when she responded to a knock at the door and beheld a tall, gray-bearded man. The man inquired did she not recognize him? He then revealed himself to be Charles Cameron, her former husband, who had come to ask for her forgiveness.

Cameron, a cousin of U.S. Senator James Donald Cameron, had married the former Mary Merkle in Pottsville in 1848. After the birth of several children, the *Herald* article reported, Cameron began to drink and neglect his family. In 1860, when their youngest child was only a month old, Cameron told his wife he was going to Richmond, Va., where he claimed to have a contract to build a church.

"In a few weeks, his wife received a letter and $20. Two more letters followed, one with $5 and another with $6 and then she heard no more from her husband. One day soon after the battle of Bull Run she was informed her husband had been stabbed to death in a gambling den in Virginia."

Later the supposed widow and her children moved to Greenbrier, where she met and married a young man named William Madden. Madden was killed on the railroad three years later. Widowed again, Mrs. Madden moved to Shamokin where she supported her family by operating the boarding house. At the time of Cameron's reappearance, one son, Wallace, still lived with her.

Mrs. Madden told the *Herald* Cameron was "no good" and she would hang herself rather than live with him again. The scoundrel was taken in—at least temporarily—by another son, Simon, who then lived on West Spruce street.

EXCURSION RIVALRY

Rivalry between the Pennsylvania and Lehigh Valley railroads led to disappointed excursion patrons and chastisement by a newspaper in October 1891.

The Pennsy advertised a special rate for an excursion to Pottsville. Prospective passengers in Shenandoah—including members of the GAR post band, 40 members of the Columbia Hose Company, and a large delegation of the

Rescue Hook and Ladder—waited a lengthy period only to be rewarded with arrival of a train already packed with passengers. The few from Shenandoah who were able to get aboard had to stand as all seats were occupied.

The *Evening Herald* of Thursday, Oct. 1, blamed the fiasco on the rivalry between the railroad companies and disclosed that Lehigh had undercut the other by selling tickets the night before on the street and directing customers to come to their depot if seats were not available on the first train.

"Scores of people said this morning that had they not been led to believe that there would be a special train at the Pennsylvania depot they would not have gone there," the *Herald* said.

"As a consequence of the bad arrangements the GAR Post, which was the prime mover in arranging for the excursion to Pottsville, together with its band and a large number of its friends, was really left behind. On the other hand, the Phoenix Hose Company and Temperance band secured seats by going to the Lehigh Valley depot."

The Pennsylvania and Reading got its rebuke, too. The newspaper said if the company did not want to lose the patronage it had it should be obliged to make better arrangements for the accommodation and comfort of the public.

An indignant passenger at the Pennsylvania depot was quoted as saying, "You may say the Pennsylvania and Reading Railroad company is slow, but I tell you it is better to be slow and sure than to make a mess of a thing."

A SPLENDID TRIP

Obviously not all excursions such as the one above benefited the average person. The railroads had to placate their investors and biggest customers, as will be seen in the following account from the June 1, 1891 issue of the Evening Herald published with the head "A Splendid Trip."

It was noted that on the previous morning two first class passenger cars of the Pennsylvania & Reading, drawn by Engine No. 449, left the depot in charge of Wellington Bartolette, assistant superintendent, and a crew comprised of

Harry Kleinhart, conductor; Charles Cook, engineer; Charles Barrett, fireman, and Fenton Thomas, brakeman.

Passengers on board included railroad and coal company dignitaries and their guests. More of these were picked up on stops at William Penn, Mahanoy Plane, and Mahanoy City.

"Then the train sped onward to Lakeside. Then to and through the romantic scenery of the Catawissa, over several high trestles to Girard Manor, where a short stop was made. Catawissa was the next stopping point and there Superintendent (C.M.) Lawler and his friend, C. Kiskadden, of Tiffin, Ohio, joined the tourists. Mr. Lawler was greeted heartily. He had traveled from Williamsport to Catawissa in his private car to join the party."

The group visited West Milton, Lewisburg, Sunbury, Shamokin, Gordon, and Ashland before returning to Shenandoah, in total a round trip of about 150 miles.

Along the way, the passengers were served refreshments by 'Billy' Lloyd, a "popular caterer."

"The trip was a most delightful one. The delightful weather, exquisite scenery and thrilling rides over the high trestles, of which there are seven between Krebs' station and Catawissa, furnished a day that will long be pleasantly remembered by the tourists."

THE CIRCUS

Arrival of a circus or carnival was always an anticipated event in patches and towns throughout the coal region, and they usually arrived by train—scores of passenger, stock, and flat railway cars to be unloaded at a siding, attracting young and old to watch the parade to the grounds where the tents would be set up.

Collieries and other industries in a town would shut down, providing a holiday for workers and their families.

"The circus is here and the small boys, the old boys, the girls, young ladies, and their mothers are reveling in a spasm of delight," declared the *Evening Herald* on May 9, 1892.

Forepaugh Circus vintage circus poster.

Adam Forepaugh's Shows arrived in Shenandoah following performances in Shamokin. "People flocked to the
grounds from town by the hundreds all day yesterday and
gazed in wonderment upon the colossal amusement plant."

Forepaugh, a Philadelphia native, had died in 1890. His
acts and trappings had been sold to the Ringling Brothers
who eventually transformed their small animal production
to the behemoth known as the Barnum & Bailey Circus.

While the clowns, aerial acts, elephants, and other
beasts bemused adults and children alike, the newspaper
also warned the public to be on guard while the circus was
in town.

"Fakirs and crooks are on hand in hundreds and too
strict a watch cannot be kept. If any families leave their
homes without occupants they should see that all windows
and doors are securely locked, and at all times a watch
should be kept for sneaks."

However, the following day the newspaper reported little
trouble associated with the circus. "There were but two arrests during the entire day, which is an excellent record.

One, a man who gave the name of M. Lewis and said he resided in Wilkes-Barre, attempted to play a shell game at the Philadelphia & Reading passenger depot.

"He was scooped in by Constable Toomey and put under bail for trial. The other party was also a fakir and he was released upon paying a fine. There were no drunks or disorderlies, no fights and no accidents, yet it is estimated that there were fully eight thousand visitors of all classes in the town during the day."

DANCING CONTEST

In the spring of 1892 the Methodist General Conference was pondering a petition seeking to expunge from the denomination's discipline section No. 242 relating to amusements, specifically seeking its modifications to permit dancing by members.

Though Methodists and some other Protestant religious organizations frowned on men and women dancing as a social activity, there was another type of dance popular throughout the coal region and deeply rooted in the Celtic origins of some of its inhabitants.

This was a competitive event between men, dependent on skill, agility, and endurance and it came with the awarding of trophies and cash prizes and was usually accompanied by gambling on the outcome.

The May 14, 1892 *Evening Herald* of Shenandoah advertised one such event to be held that evening.

"The sporting fraternity will crowd to H. J. McGuire's hotel in Girardville to-night to witness the dancing contest between David Jones, of Mt. Carmel, and James Cauley, of Lost Creek, for $25 a side. The parties are old-time rivals and the match has created considerable interest."

The same issue of the newspaper also mentioned plans for another popular sporting event of the times, a 100-yard footrace between George Ringheiser of Shenandoah and an African-American named Rooney from Wilkes-Barre to be held in Wilkes-Barre with a $200 prize at stake.

FOURTH OF JULY

The Reading Railroad announced in area newspapers in July 1892 it would, ". . . as usual, contribute to the general enjoyment of the 'Glorious Fourth' by selling special, reduced rate excursion tickets on July 1st, 2nd, 3rd and 4th, good to return until the 5th, inclusive. No special tickets will be sold where the excursion rate is less than 25 cents."

The "Glorious Fourth" was a special occasion for celebration by our ancestors, not only to express their patriotic fervor, but also because it was a legal holiday with no work for most, providing an opportunity for family and friends spread apart in different patches and towns to gather together and celebrate. And the railroad operators saw it as an opportunity to cash in by offering special rates for the travelers.

Seeing the possibility of additional sales, newspapers urged their readers—as in this example from the *Evening Herald*—". . . to confer a favor upon the publishers by forwarding the names of friends or relatives from out of town they may entertain to-day."

One visitor from another part of the commonwealth expressed surprise to a reporter that stores were closed and thought the temptation to businessmen to keep their places open when the town was so crowded must have been great. He also found the behavior of the people excellent in contrast to reports he had heard of goings on in the coal region. "He marveled that it took but five policemen to preserve order in the town with its mixed population of over 16,000. Our schools were equally surprising to him and, taking all in all, his opinion of the coal region has undergone a great change."

It was a grand day of speeches, parades, and picnics. "Here and there the people darted with flags and banners and the rap-rap of the tack hammers against the majestic buildings told the populace that the star spangled banner was being unfurled.

"The day broke with glorious patriotic fire and amid the roar of cannon and the cheers of the multitude the parade was formed in front of the hotel at 9:00 a.m."

In addition to local bands and fraternal groups, the parade that year in Shenandoah included bands and organizations from Mount Carmel, Mahanoy City, Girardville, Frackville, and Ringtown.

The celebrations did result in one less enjoyable aspect reported in the following day's paper: "In view of the promiscuous use of fireworks in town yesterday the returns of accidents are comparatively light. There were several cases in which children suffered from exploding crackers but in no instance were the injuries serious."

The account then went on to list eight such accidents.

PRACTICAL JOKERS

My dad told me about some of the practical jokes he and his buddies pulled on neighbors when he was growing up in Shamokin's Fifth Ward. One of their favorites was disassembling a junk dealer's wagon, hauling it up on a roof, and reassembling it. Antics such as he described would land a boy or man in jail these days but were a common source of fun to past generations.

An example is this one I found in the July 7, 1892 *Evening Herald*:

Some residents of South West street were very much vexed a few mornings since. When they attempted to open the front doors of their houses they found they could not do so and attempts to open the rear doors were equally fruitless.

"For a time they could not understand what was the matter, but upon looking out the windows they found that ropes had been wound about the door knobs and fastened to the neighboring knobs, so that several doors were so held that they could not be opened.

"Indignation was at a high pitch over the discovery and it did not diminish by the discovery that the locks of outhouses had been stuffed with paper. A diligent search for the mischievous parties is going on.

CAMP MEETINGS

Like revivals, camp meetings were popular events with the religiously inclined.

One such event was scheduled for the week beginning July 19, 1892 at the popular Lakeside resort under the auspices of the Pottsville District, Evangelical Association.

The Reading was offering excursion tickets from Pottsville, Port Carbon, Tamaqua, Shamokin, and other stations along the line.

The event included services for both adults and children and a special service was planned ". . . in the interests of the Christian Endeavor Society." Tents were erected on the grounds and were available at prices ranging from $3.00 to $3.75. Season tickets, including 23 meals were offered for $4.00. Day tickets cost 80 cents, breakfast and supper could be had for 24 cents each or dinner alone for 40 cents. Children under five were admitted free and those between five and 12 for half the adult price.

GYPSIES

Tramps and hoboes were a yearlong source of irritation to both the railroads and townsmen in the nineteenth century. Though some were unemployed men who rode the rails in search of work, others were prone to criminal acts, making them all subject to harassment by railroad and town police.

Gypsies, on the other hand, were spring and summer visitors who were both welcome and suspect. They were welcome because they came to sell handmade baskets and other crafts, do some horse trading, and tell fortunes. Because their lifestyle was different, they were also likely to be accused of any crime occurring during their stay in the vicinity.

Three distinct bands of gypsies, or Romany as they preferred to be known, traveled the Pennsylvania countryside. The first Romany group came to the commonwealth from the German Palatinate in the late 1720s, fleeing persecution and the poverty resulting from the Thirty Years War. These darker skinned Germans were variously known as Chi-kener (a probable corruption of the German word zigeuner, meaning gypsy) and Black Dutch. A second group migrated from the British Isles beginning in the 1850s; these are the people commonly known as Travelers in Great Britain. The third group began trickling in from Eastern Europe, particularly Hungary and Romania, in the 1880s.

Because of their unusual lifestyle, they aroused considerable curiosity in the places they visited. I found a story of a reporter in Schuylkill County who visited one of their camps in search of a story. He found a number of people willing to talk—for a price. After an exasperating time, he finally got to one man who offered to talk for free. But, just as they sat down for a talk, they were surrounded by the gypsy's kinsmen who chided him and demanded the reporter pay for the story.

Not wanting to lose the opportunity, the reporter paid in hope he would be reimbursed by his employer. He learned the band comprised of 24 individuals of English descent and four hired hands, including two African Americans. The man being interviewed had been born in Dayton, Ohio, while a brother was born in Indiana. They had 30 head of horses they hoped to sell or trade in area towns before moving on.

They declined to discuss any more exotic practices to the reporter's chagrin.

COUNCIL BRAWL

Political disagreements often cause tempers to flare. Fortunately, it less often escalates to violence.

Henry "Snapper" Reese, who served with distinction during the Civil War, migrated from Schuylkill County to Shamokin where he became, first, chief of police, and then burgess. He was serving in this latter capacity one evening in the fall of 1892 when he came close to blows with a city councilman and former railroader. The incident occurred on Tuesday, Sept. 6, 1892.

An article in the Friday, Sept. 9, issue of the *Shamokin Herald* stated, "Burgess Reese and Frederic Lorenz were the disputants and while standing face to face doubled their dukes and would have let drive at each other had not Al Weaver sprang from his chair and passed between the angry men."

Lorenz, a civil engineer who came to Shamokin and worked in the construction of various branches for the Philadelphia and Reading Railway Company, later worked for the First National Bank and became active in community affairs, serving both on council and the city school board.

Henry "Snapper" Reese (Obit photo from newspaper.)

The newspaper said Reese was angered when Lorenz denounced him for his way of doing things "in opposition" to councils' will during a tirade on work planned for Chestnut street. "Reese grew red and ordered Lorenz to sit down. The latter declined, stating he had the floor. 'I have the floor,' cried that gentleman, with which he delivered a volley of hot shot straight at the hero of Petersburg. The latter trained his artillery and for a few moments the cannonading was terrific.

"Different members offered counsel, requesting the two to calm down and the angry men finally took their seats. Tempers flared again when Lorenz proposed a resolution binding actions by Reese. The resolution failed."

DECORATING ADVICE

The *Evening Herald* of Shenandoah, Schuylkill County, offered some advice for its readers on trimming Christmas trees in the Saturday, Dec. 24, 1892 edition.

The newspaper urged parents to allow children to help in decorating.

"The trimming of the Christmas tree is such an important holiday ceremony that it is a pity the children are not allowed to help or see the tree until it is ready. It would seem as if they might share more truly the Christmas spirit if they assisted at the trimming, their gifts being tied on when they are not around, and then if they choose share the tree with some less fortunate playmates after it has been stripped on Christmas Eve or Christmas Day for themselves."

The newspaper also declared, "The prettiest kind of tree is that which contains the most ornaments that glitter, and the most candles to show them well."

Many families in that time period made their own ornaments, using gilt or silver paper to make chains or strings of popcorn which could also be embellished with gilt or other coloring. The use of open candles on the limbs of the tree was a common, though dangerous, practice. The *Herald* suggested piling cotton batten around the base of the tree to give the semblance of a snow drift, which could also be enhanced with a dusting of glitter.

For those who could not afford to purchase a tree, the *Herald* proposed a Christmas trunk. "It will be less trouble and scarcely any expense. Put all the gifts, done up in packages and properly labeled, into any convenient trunk, a flat top one being best. Tack over the outside of the trunk cotton batting, sprinkled, if possible, with diamond dust. A rope of Christmas green is fastened around the edge of the lid and around the bottom of the trunk. Have the cotton at the edge of the lid hang down like a fringe, so that when the lid is lifted it will hang over several inches. Line the lid with dark green stuff or paper in the centre of which are the words, 'Merry Christmas,' in gilt letters. The rest of the green may be sprinkled with gold stars."

FREE LUNCH FIASCO

Two feuding saloon keepers in Shenandoah learned a lesson on generosity in October 1893.

The *Evening Herald* reported on Oct. 18 the two were attempting to outdo one another in enticing customers by providing free lunches when their rivalry backfired and began costing them more than they were making.

"Both places did a good business until very recently, neither being engaged in the free lunch business. One day, about three weeks ago, one of the saloonkeepers decided to attract some of his rival's trade, and the following day his patrons were surprised to see a free lunch spread out for them."

After a few days as the other witnessed his customers being drawn away, he retaliated by advertising a better fare than that offered by his rival. The two upped the ante over a period of time.

"Then came the next step. The other one dressed a waiter up in snow white apron and cap, stationed him behind the lunch counter, which was plentifully stocked with hams, cold meats, cheese, crackers, sandwiches and other eatables, and gave orders that each applicant at the counter should get all he wanted to eat. And again this saloonkeeper became the most popular man of the neighborhood."

But his victory lasted only a day until his opponent quit.

"On his free lunch, after indulging in one glass of beer, an ordinary man can make a good meal, and hundreds are doing so daily at small cost. And the hungry and thirsty are praying each night that the feud may grow in bitterness, while the free lunch grows in quantity."

TRAVELING SHOWS AND VAUDEVILLE

Traveling shows and vaudeville were much anticipated and well-attended diversions in small and large communities. An advertisement in the Jan. 19, 1895 issue of the *Evening Herald* advised the public on what awaited them in a coming performance:

> Daisey Beverly, supported by her own talented company, appearing in the romantic melodrama in four acts, 'Silver Bird,' an exquisite story of heart and home, sparkling with wit, humor and merriment. At Ferguson's theatre on Tuesday evening, January 22d.

The Beverly company included Little Pansy, "the wonderful and bewitching child actress;" the Shetland pony Price and trotting dog Spot who "display almost human intelligence in playing their respective parts."

The day following the performance, the *Herald* commented that the show was "well patronized and gave general satisfaction."

"The play is of the regulation border type, but clever acting of Daisey Beverly and Little Pansy raise it above the ordinary productions. The company carries a good orchestra with it."

ADDED ATTRACTION

A visit of Buffalo Bill's Wild West Show to Scranton on May 10, 1895 had an added attraction for those who attended the evening performance.

"At night the scene is one that will be long remembered," the *Scranton Tribune* reported. "A chance will be given the public to see the latest invention of the scientific age, that of a portable electric light plant with a capacity of 250,000 candle power, which makes the field in which the performance is given as bright as in the daytime, and the effect is more pleasing than can be imagined."

This was the first time Colonel William F. Cody and his show visited the Electric City and the *Tribune* began its report by calling it "one of the most novel sights that has ever been witnessed," adding, "There is an impression that the Wild West show is a circus, but those who have made up their minds to that should change it, as there is as much difference as there is difference between a vaudeville entertainment and a performance of 'Hamlet' by a good tragedian."

WHEELMEN MEET

Bicycling as a means of sport, pleasure, and transportation was growing at a fast rate in the 1890s. Many enthusiasts formed clubs. One such group, the Green Ridge Wheelmen held a smoker on May 9, 1895 in their clubhouse.

"The West End Wheelmen of Wilkes-Barre were invited but failed to attend," the *Scranton Tribune* reported. "Nevertheless about one hundred of the club members were present and spent a most enjoyable evening.

"Mandolin and guitar music was furnished by Mssrs. Curtis, Ross and Schapert. M.J. Coyne whistled several selections in his original manner, eliciting rounds of applause. A lunch was served about 11 o'clock."

RENOUNCED A FORTUNE

Despite opposition from her father, a Pottsville heiress renounced a fortune and married her lover, a common railroad laborer, on Jan. 27, 1898.

The sub-head on the Jan. 28 story in the *Philadelphia Inquirer* proclaimed in bold print: "Love Found A Way." In a special report to the *Inquirer*, a reporter wrote: "A big sensation was created in the social circles of this place over the wedding of Edward A. Ratigan and Miss Mary E. Drumheller."

The bride was the only daughter of Jesse Drumheller, a borough councilman and director of the Pennsylvania Bank, whose worth was estimated at over a quarter million dollars. Ratigan was a laborer employed in the Pottsville railroad shops. The newspaper article described him as being of "very prepossessing appearance."

The report said the heiress first saw the groom several months earlier while he was playing with the Third Brigade Band and became infatuated with him. "The lovers met and decided to wed despite the bitter opposition of the bride's father, who threatened to disinherit her if she did not break off her engagement with Ratigan.

"After the wedding today Mr. Drumheller tore up his will, which read in her favor, and says he will cut off his daughter without a cent. Miss Drumheller is much attached to her new husband, whom she prefers to the fortune which would have been her portion."

The report concluded by saying Drumheller had sold at a loss a $50,000 hotel he'd been holding for his daughter. The father said he was disappointed in his child and would shut his doors to her in protest of her defiance.

The 1900 census shows the couple residing in Pottsville's Third Ward with two daughters and Ratigan's occupation listed as musician. They are found in later census with additional children, indicating it was a case of true love.

OTHER DIVERSIONS

An ad of a type seen often in old newspapers:

"Five thousand novels, the latest and best issued, selling at 25 cents other places, for sale at Max Reese's for 10 cents. The finest playing cards in the market, 5 cents per pack."

People did read, play cards, and enjoy a variety of board games in those days.

COMING EVENTS

Advertised in a summer edition of the *Evening Herald* were these:

July 9—Picnic for the benefit of Andrew Highland, at the St. Nicholas band grove.

July 16—Raspberry and ice cream festival, Robbins' opera house, for the benefit of the Sons of Veterans Light Infantry.
July 18—Ice cream festival and bean soup lunch, Robbins' opera house, under the auspices of the Womens' Relief Corps.

July 22—Strawberry and ice cream festival, in Robbins' opera house, under the auspices of Young America Drum Corps.

FISHING WOES

A decline of fish in the North Branch of the Susquehanna River in 1904 led to speculation coal dirt might be to blame, though a fisherman disputed the idea.

"The North Branch in this vicinity several years ago was one of the best fishing grounds in this section," the *Danville Intelligencer* reported on Sept. 9, 1904. "Of late years, however, it has yielded very poor sport, each succeeding year seeming to bring fewer fish.

"A well known fisherman of our town stated yesterday that a few years ago it was no unusual thing for him to hook as many as four hundred bass in a season, while during the present year he has thus far caught but fourteen.

"During the last few years when the falling off in the fish was first noted, black bass were still plentiful in the West

Branch, which gave rise to the theory that the fish in the North Branch were beginning to suffer from the inroads of coal dirt. It now develops that black bass have become as scarce in the West Branch as anywhere else, so that the fishermen are beginning to look for some cause for the general scarcity other than coal dirt."

The fisherman quoted in the article surmised ice gorges and a big flood the previous spring had swept large numbers of fish downstream and they were prevented from returning by dams lower down the river.

FRATERNAL GROUPS

From the smallest town to the large cities, Americans eagerly joined fraternal orders in droves—and the coal region and railroaders were not exceptions to this desire to affiliate with others with similar interests.

B. H. Meyer, a sociologist who studied the subject in the early twentieth century, estimated there were nearly 600 fraternal beneficiary societies in the United States with a membership of five and a half million.[1]

These groups ranged from the more familiar Masonic, Odd Fellows, and similar organizations still in existence to obscure and long forgotten clubs.

Meyer found they all had three general features: they filled a social need for people with a common interest; they had a defined ritual (often kept secret from the public), and, most importantly, financial assistance to members in sickness and destitution. Members paid an admission fee of from a dollar to $50 and annual dues ranging from $2 to $10. Some organizations had auxiliaries, others did not.

This last feature was most important in a time when social benefits from employers and government were limited. It is for this reason many of the organizations affiliated with insurance companies to assure money would be available when needed. Meyer said one of the organizations included

---

1. Fraternal Beneficiary Societies in the United States, American Journal of Sociology, Vol. 6, B.H. Meyer, 1902

in his study had paid out in excess of three million dollars in the previous year for the relief of brothers and families.

The 1902 Sears, Roebuck catalog has a page of secret society and lodge emblem charms for sale. Among those offered were pins for Masonic orders, Odd Fellows, Independent Order of Foresters, Knights of Pythias, GAR (Grand Army of the Republic), Sons of Veterans, Ancient Order United Workmen, Modern Woodmen, Order of Redmen, United American Mechanics, and Knights of the Maccabees.

MISSED THE GAME

Desire to see a World Series baseball game in Philadelphia landed two Shamokin youths in trouble with the law in the autumn of 1911 after they encountered a railroad policeman.

The incident was reported in the Tuesday, Oct. 24, 1911 issue of the *Patriot*, Harrisburg.

John Lalhe (name as spelled in the newspaper) and William Morgan, ages 14 and 13, were taken into custody at the Union station in Harrisburg by a railroad officer when he found them hitching a ride on the bumpers of a baggage coach.

When apprehended, the boys informed the officer of their intention.

"Well, don't you know that it is against the law to ride on a train that way?" asked the officer. "Besides look at the danger you boys were in. Suppose you would have fallen off, and been killed what do you think your parents would have done?"

One of the boys responded he guessed they wouldn't have seen a game in that case.

The youths were given a choice of being sent back to their parents or going to jail. The newspaper reported they were returned to their parents on Oct. 23.

The reporter noted he overheard one say to the other, "Ain't this tough luck? After we have been saving every penny we got just to see one of those games then running right into the hands of the cops here."

4

ON THE JOB

ON CALL

When I was a boy we moved to Tharptown, just outside Shamokin, a village in a narrow valley, flanked on one side by the tracks of the Reading and on the other by those of the Pennsy. The sounds and sight of passing freights on both lines was a regular occurrence. Today I reside again in the same house, but the Reading's tracks are gone and the Pennsy's are used only sporadically by the North Shore, a short line running out of Union County.

I miss the passage of those old steamers and the diesels that supplanted them, though I'm glad when I hear the horn and rumble of the North Shore and it calls to mind memories of those days of my youth.

At some point dad acquired a couple lots in the country and considered building a new house there. His job depended on having a telephone so the dispatcher could alert him to his schedule. When dad discovered Ma Bell had no line poles near his property and he would have to pay a fee for every pole needed to run a telephone line to the vicinity, he decided he couldn't afford it and disposed of the land and the idea of building. We remained in Tharptown.

Dad worked himself up from the menial positions of crossing guard and track crewman to, successively, the more prestigious and better paying positions of fireman, brakeman, and conductor. He began work in the 1930s when the railroad was still a major player in the transportation industry and ended his forty-plus year career after Congress swept a number of bankrupt railroads into the federally-supported Conrail system.

CALLBOYS

Before Alexander Graham Bell's invention gave dispatchers a means to contact and assemble crews, men were summoned to work by bicycle-riding youths known as callboys.

Armed with a notebook containing the names and addresses of employees (or the boarding houses where they slept), a pencil, and lantern, these youngsters would be sent out, night or day, in good and bad weather, to find and alert the crew of when and where to report for duty.

I'm not aware of any of my ancestors getting their start this way, but most callboys came from railroading families and it was a time-honored means of stepping up to a better job with the company. As folklorist George Korson noted in the section on railroaders in Pennsylvania Songs and Legends, "*Who's Who in Railroading* is replete with the names of officials who started out with a scarred bike and little black book, the autograph of trainmen and enginemen, but came to know the right people and gradually climbed the ladder."[1]

Bell may have taken their jobs, but the telephone didn't prevent young men from finding other ways to land a job on the railroad.

GANDY DANCERS

Before a train could run, someone had to lay the tracks and ties on which the tracks rest.

Robert Livingston Stevens, son of Colonel John Stevens, designed the prototype of the modern T-rail for his Camden & Amboy line. These first American-designed iron rails were rolled in 1844. Earlier American trains ran on tracks of wood topped with a metal strap.

Section gangs, workers often referred to as gandy dancers, were the laborers responsible for laying and maintaining the tracks.

This was a low-paying job requiring brawn more than brains and in the earliest years of railroading, recent

---

1. Pennsylvania Songs and Legends, George Korson, editor, University of Pennsylvania Press, Philadelphia, 1949.

immigrants and ethnic minorities—pleased to have steady work and less concerned about working conditions than native Americans—were the obvious choice for employment. In the east these jobs fell in turn to the Irish, Poles, Italians, and other European immigrants as well as African-Americans. In the west, the laborers were most often Chinese or Mexican.

Under the direction of a roadmaster, these men would lay down and tamp a bed of stone, followed by the creosoted wooden ties on which the tracks rested. Over time, the vibration of passing trains would cause shifts in the tracks. If these shifts were neglected, they had the potential to eventually cause a derailment.

To prevent this problem, track crews would regularly need to realign the tracks. This was accomplished with a lining bar, five feet or more in length, each man using his tool in a team effort to force the track back in place.

In addition to inspecting and correcting rail and tie problems, crews regularly rebuilt washed-out roadbeds and handled other maintenance tasks.

Some theorize the lining bar and its use is the source of the term gandy dancer because the movement of the workers lunging against their bars resembled a dance move. The earliest printed reference to the term dates to 1918.[2]

Other tools employed by these workmen included picks and shovels, sledge hammers, rail dogs (tongs used to carry rails), and chisels.

There are some reports that the Reading employed women on track crews due to a shortage of men during World War II. Modern machinery, such as spike-driving machines, later replaced much of the needed manpower.

SHOPMEN

Some 400,000 men were employed by U.S. railroads by 1880 and one authority estimates 20 percent of them worked in the shops, constructing and maintaining locomotives, freight cars, and other rolling stock.[3]

---

2. The Outlook magazine, New York, May 1918.
3. Working for the Railroad: The Organization of Work in the Nineteenth Century, Walter Licht, Princeton University Press, New Jersey, 1983.

These men included machinists, blacksmiths, carpenters, mechanics, and apprentices in those and related crafts.

The importance of these workers to the industry can't be underestimated. An article in the *Sunbury American* on Saturday, Feb. 18, 1854 noted: "A good Locomotive Engine costs from $9,000 to $10,500, and it would take nine men a whole year to build one well, with all the machine power of the best machine-shop to aid them in the work."

An eight-wheel engine was patented on Feb. 6, 1837 by Henry R. Campbell of Philadelphia and, with additional modifications, this American type of locomotive remained the most popular until the mid-1890s.

The Evening Herald, Shenandoah, reported on Sept. 10, 1891,"Engine 577, a dirt-burner, built by the Lehigh Valley Railroad Company at Weatherly, recently handled 101 gondola cars equal to 303 ordinary six-ton coal cars from Bethlehem to Packertown in three hours. This is the greatest haul yet recorded on the Lehigh Division."

These behemoths were the mainstay of the coal region railroads and they could not roll without them and the other stock built, serviced, and maintained by the shopmen.

A work stoppage over a pay dispute by shopmen in 1920, one of the largest nationwide strikes of railroad workers in the U.S., nearly crippled the industry before being settled. This will be discussed in more detail in a section on labor.

"Mr. H. V. Poor, a most experienced and sober statistician, and a first-class authority on the railroads of the United States, calculates that new railroads have been built, during the last twenty years, in this country, at the rate of two thousand miles a year; that this is to be three thousand miles a year hereafter, and more too; that the whole length of railroads now in operation in the United States is (on January 1, 1870) forty-seven thousand miles."[4]

Those numbers provide some insight into why the shopman was so important to the industry.

In addition to the locomotives, (a majority of those used by the coal region companies manufactured by the

---

4. The Great Industries of the United States, Horace Greeley et al, J.B. Burr & Hyde, Hartford, Conn., 1872.

celebrated Baldwin Works of Philadelphia) there were also the other cars to be maintained. None of them came cheap.

Estimates are that a flat car cost upwards of $600 while one of ". . . those gorgeous traveling hotels called 'Palace Cars'" might cost as much as $20,000.

The following little table shows the approximate weight and cost of different styles of cars:

DESIGNATION OF CAR	WEIGHT, LBS.	COST
Pullman	56,000	$12,000-20,000
Passenger	39,000	$5,000-6,000
Do. 2nd class	35,000	$3,000-4,000
Freight (box)	16,000	$700-800
Flat or platform	12,000	$550-650[5]

TRAIN CREWS

In the nineteenth and early twentieth century, most freight trains operated with a crew of five persons—a conductor, two brakemen, the engineer, and a fireman.

FIREMAN

In the days of steam, the fireman was essentially the co-pilot of the train and worked in teamwork with the engineer in running the locomotive.

His primary responsibility was managing the output of steam by keeping the firebox fed with coal and controlling the water temperature in the boiler. Generally he didn't actually build the fire since it took hours for a proper heat to be attained and the fire would have been built by some other employee before he came on duty.

Once on board, he had the additional job of helping keep the engineer alert to signals, grade, and track changes. If he had hopes of promotion he might be allowed to take a hand at the throttle at times under the watchful eye of his engineer.

---

5. The Great Industries, etc.

With the advent of the diesel, the fireman's duties diminished and eventually the job was phased out.

ENGINEER

One might assume the engineer was "captain" of the train, but that was not the case. The engineer worked under a number of bosses, starting with the conductor of the train. The engineer also answered to a road foreman in addition to trainmasters, yardmasters, dispatchers, and also the roundhouse foreman—all of them together responsible for the safety and efficiency of the run.

In the cab, the engineer had to control the speed of his massive vehicle and work in coordination with the fireman and other crew to maintain safe control of the train.

BRAKEMAN

Another vital element of the crew, these men were responsible for throwing switches, attending to hand brakes when cars are separated from a train, coupling and uncoupling cars, watching for potential hazards, and flagging (signaling with flags) should they spot a conflict with another train.

The head brakeman usually rode in the engine with the engineer and fireman while his counterpart was onboard the caboose.

These men also answered directly to the conductor, but also reported to the trainmaster.

CONDUCTOR

The conductor was responsible for his crew and train. He reported directly to the trainmaster and got his orders from the dispatcher and yardmasters.

He didn't simply sit in the caboose and give orders. His job required him to be all over the train to assure everything was in order. The job required intelligence, stamina, and physical abilities since, in a crux, he might be called upon to set brakes or handle other duties generally tended by the crew.

Rising to the position of conductor required experience in the other positions and the passage of rigid examinations to ascertain the abilities of the applicant. I have some of dad's notebooks he used in studying for brakeman and, later, conductor and it's apparent the tests weren't easy, multiple-choice examinations.

These were the primary jobs on the freights on which many of my ancestors worked. In addition to these, positions on a passenger train also included a chief of services, stewards, chef and dining car assistants, and lounge, coach, and sleeping car attendants.

A SPY

A "spy" was blamed in March 1890 for levying false charges which were jeopardizing the jobs of Shamokin railroaders.

The Reading Railroad had on the books for many years a rule that any employee guilty of drinking intoxicating beverages would be summarily discharged. Austin Corwin, who succeeded Franklin Benjamin Gowen as president of the railroad, felt the law was not being enforced and ordered a crackdown.

These Shamokin residents received dismissal notices on March 27: William Gensil, fireman; Charles Gibberson, engineer; Harry McElwee, fireman; John Weiser, fireman; Peter Haines, engineer; Albert Bleach, engineer, and Sherman Booth, fireman.

The notices came from William Williams, superintendent of the Reading roundhouse at Shamokin on behalf of G. S. Allen, master mechanic, Tamaqua.

Ironically, the *Shamokin Herald* reported on March 28, 1890 that none of the men had reputations as drinkers. In fact, several were known as non-drinkers and all of the men claimed they never drank on duty. They unanimously voiced intent to seek legal counsel and demanded a hearing. The *Herald* reported:

"Harry McElwee is the son of John McElwee, trainmaster on the Northern Central railroad, and is a devout member of the Methodist church. He has not been inside a saloon the eighteen months he worked for the Reading company and never tasted liquor except when his father gave it to him while he was sick in bed during his childhood days. The young man will likely bring action against the Reading company for defamation of character.

"Gardner Cobb has been with the company twenty-two years and was one of their most trusted men. Two drinks passed his lips in five years.

"Peter Haines is a Methodist church member and drinks not a drop. His friend Sherman Booth is a sober, industrious Christian, being a member of the same church. He has not tasted liquor for a long time."

Contacted by the newspaper, one company official claimed 24 Shamokin brakemen had been fired for drinking on the job. Yet another said only one, a man named Harry Kleckner was dismissed. Kleckner, described as "an intelligent young man with an honest look," told a reporter he did not drink and was mystified and grieved over his firing.

Area railroaders pointed the finger of suspicion at a man named James C. Head who had been in town several weeks earlier, making inquiries about Reading men.

The *Herald* said, "Head was about 28 years old and of Irish descent. He was possessed of a hatchet face and talked with some intelligence." It was noted he came to the newspaper office and asked that his business be kept out of print. "It is said that he was severely beaten at Tamaqua last night by railroaders for trying to get them to put their autographs on fancy cards he produced."

Apparently a number of the accused men were able to clear their names, as they are found back on the job in the 1900 census.

THOSE RULES AGAIN

The Pennsylvania and Reading issued a new book of rules for its employees, which were to go into effect on the 15th, including some that had not existed previously, it was reported in the May 12, 1892 *Evening Herald*.

It appears the railroad may have been under pressure from the temperance forces.

"Uniformed employees, passenger train employees, shop men, passenger train locomotive engineers and firemen, clerks and such other employees as may be designated by the heads of departments, will not be permitted to smoke on duty, neither will passenger train conductors, brakemen, station agents, or telegraph operators be permitted to use tobacco in any form while upon duty in the presence of the public."

Drunkenness on or off duty was also forbidden.

Another rule called for the suspension or dismissal of an employee who allowed his wages to be attached for a board bill.

Trainmen were also required to have their watches examined every six months by a "responsible" watchmaker, who was to provide a certificate stating the watch was reliable. "These certificates must be filed before a conductor and engineer will be given a train or engine," the rule book said.

5

ACCIDENTS

A DANGEROUS PROFESSION

It's obvious to all, coal mining and railroading are dangerous occupations. But, surprisingly, an 1897 report indicates working on the railroad was the more dangerous job—at least in that year.

The report compiled by the Interstate Commerce Commission was published in the November 20 edition of *The Evening Item* of Sunbury.

According to the report, the number of railway employees killed during the year ending June 30, 1897 was 1,861, an increase of 50 over the previous year. The number injured was listed as 29,969, up 4,273 from the year before.

The number of passengers killed was 181 and the number injured was 2,783 (an increase of 11 over the previous year).

"This report shows that the risk of passengers is very small, but that the train hands occupy very dangerous positions," the newspaper noted. The report included a ratio based upon miles traveled which indicated 72,093,963 passenger miles were accomplished for every passenger killed and 4,541,945 miles for every passenger injured.

In addition to employees and passengers, the report listed 4,406 killed and 5,845 injured, which included persons reported as trespassers, of whom 3,811 were killed and 4,468 were injured.

The casualties ratio revealed that for every 444 men employed on the railroad, one was killed and for every 28 men employed, one was injured.

The ICC statistics showed that for the same time period in 1897, the number of employees in Pennsylvania coal mines killed was 342 and the number injured was 151. The report said the ratio of fatal accidents to train hands was 125 percent greater than those to coal mine employees and the ratio for non-fatal accidents was 1,510 percent greater.

However, it added, owing to "the greater dangers of anthracite mining and certain dangerous natural conditions incident to Pennsylvania's bituminous mines," the ratio of accidents to number of employees in the commonwealth was larger than in any other state.

Despite its obvious hazards, railroading had a certain status among the public. Engineers were idolized as adventurous heroes and all the employees were envied as men who had a job for life (provided they followed the rules) in contrast with most who labored on a day-to-day basis.

KILLED BY HIS SON

John Samuel Lindermuth 2nd, my great-grandfather, was the victim of a railroad accident, and his son was the engineer on the train that killed him.

John S. was born at Schuylkill Haven on Sept. 23, 1854, a son of John Samuel and Sarah (Ream) Lindermuth. Earlier in life he worked on the Schuylkill Canal, taking coal to New York, and in the brick factories at Schuylkill Haven before taking a job with the P&R which brought him to Alaska, Mount Carmel Township, and then Shamokin.

A report in the Nov. 5, 1912 edition of the *Pottsville Republican* said:

"Killed Greeting Son"
While waving a greeting to his son, Charles, who is an
engineer running between Tamaqua and Shamokin, John
Lindermuth of Shamokin, a roundhouse employee of the
Reading at that place, was crushed between a car and the
wall of the building, and so badly injured that he died a short
time later.

John and his wife, Mary Ellen (Becker) Lindermuth are buried in Old Jerusalem Cemetery, Schuylkill Haven. They were the parents of 11 known children.

I remember Great-Uncle Charles as a jovial, good-natured man and was not aware of the nature of his father's death until after his passing. Though it was clearly an unfortunate accident, I can only imagine what an effect it must have had on the son's life as he grappled with grief and guilt.

ANOTHER ANCESTOR

Though not a railroader, Jeremiah D. Reed, another ancestor, also died as a result of an accident involving a locomotive.

Jeremiah, believed to have been the first white child born at Pottsville, was a coal dealer, water company superintendent, and one-time sheriff of Schuylkill County. His father and my fourth-great-grandmother were siblings.

An account written by a grandson (later verified by a newspaper report) said Jeremiah, at the time of his death, May 27, 1881, was superintendent of the Pottsville Water Company. He was returning from the company's reservoir and was standing on the platform of the P&R depot at St. Clair, waiting for a train. As the train arrived, the cylinder head of the locomotive blew out and a piece of the metal struck him behind the left ear, killing him instantly.[1]

ENGINEER KILLED

Boiler explosions were not unusual, especially in the early days of railroading. The engineer and fireman were killed and other crew members seriously injured when the boiler of an engine exploded in May 1869.

The accident was reported in the Monday, May 10, 1869 issue of the *Shamokin Herald* and more details were released Saturday, May 15, in *The Patriot*, Harrisburg, after a jury found the Reading and Philadelphia and Erie Railroad companies blameless in the accident.

---

1. Genealogy of Walter Reed Jenkins, Pottsville PA, 1917.

The engine had been pushing a train of 31 loaded cars up the Locust Gap junction at the time of the accident. Killed were Jacob Pfeifer, engineer, and Daniel Baldy, fireman. The newspapers said injuries to Henry Boughner, John Gable, David M. Snyder, and Peter Sarvis, who were standing off to the side of the engine, were "severe, but not dangerous," consisting of scalds and bruises to the body, limbs, and face.

"Through a wonderful interposition of Providence," *The Patriot* said, "these men escaped death. Until within a few minutes of the catastrophe, they had occupied positions on the boiler, but Mr. Gable wishing to send a letter back to the Brady colliery, descended for the purpose of handing it to a person passing at the time, without knowing why the others followed, and had barely reached the fire box when the explosion occurred."

The inquest jury examined the wreck and took testimony from employees and witnesses of the incident, including master mechanics who said the boiler of the engine was in good condition and capable of bearing the maximum amount of steam to the square inch authorized by rules and regulations. It was believed the explosion ". . . was caused by an undue and over pressure of steam upon the inner surface of the said boiler, arising from some cause to the jurors unknown."

ANIMAL HAZARDS

Aside from equipment failure, one of the more dangerous hazards for railroaders was that of animals wandering onto the tracks.

Some insight into the situation is disclosed in an interview with an unidentified locomotive engineer in the July 15, 1892 edition of the *Shamokin Herald*. It might be supposed the greatest danger would be in hitting a large animal. The engineer had a different opinion.

Though different animals posed varying degrees of threat, he declared the most dreaded animals were goats and hogs.

"Of all animals that wander along the railroad track," the engineer said, "goats are the most irritating. Cows and horses are generally disposed of with ease, though sometimes they get under the wheels and cause a bad wreck. But they are so large that the pilot gets under them and throws them to one side.

"The goat, though, nearly always succeeds in getting us worked up to a high pitch of nervousness and then contrives to get off without a scratch, and that's what we don't like. No matter how fast you may be running or how quietly you steal down upon him, Mister Goat will see you out of the corner of his eye and manage to get out of the way just in time to miss the cowcatcher as the engine rushes by him."

He considered the hog the most dangerous threat to safety.

"Nine chances out of ten the hog will throw you. He is tough and greasy, you know, and if an engineer has any show at all it's best to stop the train as quick as can be and drive the animal off the track.

"When the pilot of an engine hits a hog it usually knocks him down and then rolls him for a few yards before the trucks strike him, and when they do there's great danger of their leaving the rails. The drivers are almost certain to follow the tracks, and if you don't go down the bank you're lucky. So you see what havoc one pig can make with a railroad."

He called sheep 'pitiful.'

"They seem to realize the danger they are in and huddle together between the rails, awaiting death. Their innocent eyes stare at you so mournfully and sadly that they haunt you for days to come."

"I struck a flock of geese once," he recalled, "all squatted down over the ties. Well, I never thought there were so many feathers in the world. I couldn't see anything for feathers for ten minutes, and when we reached the station my engine looked as if it had received a coat of tar and feathers."

BOILER EXPLOSION

Five men were killed and another seriously injured when a P&R locomotive exploded on Nov. 14, 1892 near Pottsville.

The *Pottsville Republican* said the engine was an L class, Number 563, and identified the victims as Henry C. Allison,

44, of Palo Alto, the engineer; Charles J. C. Mackey, 28, Port Carbon, fireman; Charles H. Kendrick, 32, Port Carbon, conductor; William Cowhey, 59, Mount Carbon, engineer of locomotive No. 73; William H. Moyer, 26, Palo Alto, fireman of Engine No. 73. Michael Dobbins, Mount Carbon, was scalded and listed in critical condition.

"The ill-fated engine with a long draught of empty cars and manned by Engineer Allison and Fireman Mackey were on their way from Port Richmond to Palo Alto and after arriving near the overhead bridge of the Lehigh and Schuylkill Valley Railroad, a short distance this side of Connor's Crossing, the locomotive exploded with the above horrifying results."

Cowhey and Moyer, who had returned their engine to the Cressona roundhouse after a trip to Reading, were hitching a ride home on Number 563.

An old railroader gave the *Republican* a theory on the cause of this and other explosions the line had recently experienced: "He said in substance the crews are compelled to run their engines at a very high temperature to draw the very heavy trains which are put behind them for the past year. To keep up the great pressure of steam and the quantity used the fires are forced and the exteriors of the boilers are burned out and something must give way."

WILD ANIMALS ON THE LOOSE

Five men were killed, numerous others injured, and 16 cages of wild animals set loose when a train bearing the Walter L. Main Circus to its next performance was wrecked May 30, 1893 near Altoona.

The *Evening Herald*, Shenandoah, reported, "The shows were being transported from Houtzdale to Lewistown, via the Tyrone and Clearfield branch of the Pennsylvania railroad, and were filling dates eastward, with a schedule that called for their arrival here on the morning of June 5th." Main had sent a telegram to the *Herald*, stating it would be impossible to finish the season.

"Within a radius of sixty square feet nothing but dead animals and debris can be seen," the *Herald* reported.

Those killed in the accident were William Henry, Tyrone, brakeman; Frank Brain, Indianapolis, Ind.; William Murperly, East Liberty, Pa.; John Stayer, Houtzdale, Pa., and Louis Champlain, Rochester, N.Y.

Of the 16 animals that had escaped, a lioness, a panther, and a tiger remained at large. "One tiger entered the yard of Alfred Thomas, a farmer, when the wife was about to milk their two cows. The tiger, a Bengal beast, leaped on one of the cows and killed it."

Commenting on Main's situation, the article concluded, "He had a good circus, but has experienced bad luck ever since leaving winter quarters until Bellefonte was reached last Saturday. He had only put up a dry canvas five times, and just two weeks ago the dressing tent was burned at Johnstown."

QUICK-THINKING AVERTS TRAGEDY

Quick thinking by a brakeman narrowly averted an accident between a Shamokin passenger train and a coal freight on Friday, May 12, 1893 at Shenandoah.

The *Evening Herald* reported the incident occurred shortly after 9:00 a.m. after a Pottsville train had pulled up to the switches on the east bound track and the coal train ran up to the Lehigh Valley depot on the west-bound track.

"The latter train was running slow when the engineer perceived the Shamokin passenger east-bound train rounding the curve south of Centre street. He opened the throttle suddenly and the coal train's speed was greatly increased, so that it soon disappeared around the curve. It was evidently the engineer's idea to get out of the way to leave the Shamokin passengers a clear road from their train to the depot, but in suddenly increasing his speed he broke the coupling of the last car—a gondola—and just as the passengers were alighting from the Shamokin train the gondola approached the depot at a rapid rate.

"The alighting passengers were warned by shouts of the train hands and people on the platform, and also by the whistle of the passenger train engine. There was a brakeman

Lehigh Depot 1940's

Lehigh depot vintage postcard.

on the gondola and he succeeded in bringing it to a stand-still just as it reached the depot."

The newspaper said the coal train engineer was unaware of what had happened and continued on his journey. He was informed by telegraph to wait at Brownsville and the brake-man, who wasn't identified or credited for his good work, ran the gondola down the grade to reunite with his train.

The *Herald* said this was not the first time a serious ac-cident had been narrowly averted. "Unless the railroad com-pany takes steps to alter its present system of running trains to and from the depot at the hour when the incident referred to occurred there will someday be a disastrous accident." It was noted four passenger trains made connections at the depot daily between 8:52 and 9:08 a.m. "There is certainly cause for apprehension when to this danger is added the running of coal trains between the passenger."

VANDALISM

An unidentified vandal was blamed for an accident involv-ing a Lehigh Valley train on Saturday, Jan. 12, 1895 near the Packer No. 4 colliery. Fortunately, there were no serious injuries.

Passenger train No. 237, drawn by engine No. 612, left Shenandoah headed for Ashland and carrying a full allotment of passengers, most of them women bound to the collieries along the route to collect wages owed their husbands or other kin.

"As the train approached Packer colliery No. 4 at a lively rate of speed it was suddenly thrown from the main line to a side track," the *Evening Herald* reported. "The engineer quickly reversed the engine and applied the air brakes, but before the train could be stopped it forced the engine against an empty gondola. The train stopped so suddenly that several passengers were thrown from their seats."

Several women suffered bruises and cuts and the engineer, Al Dent, went into shock and had to be sent home.

The engine and gondola were severely damaged. The *Herald* said the pilot was demolished and one of the steam chests knocked off. Another engine had to be provided to complete the run.

"An investigation has convinced the railway officials that the misplaced switch was due to pure maliciousness, but no clue has been obtained to the guilty party.

"The local freight and accommodation train passed the switch half an hour before the collision without mishap. Within the brief interval somebody turned the switch and escaped without detection."

TRAIN WRECKERS

Mischievous children were another hazard railroaders faced.

Two brothers, aged seven and nine, and another seven-year-old boy were arrested Monday, July 3, 1899 on suspicion of having caused a train wreck near Shamokin in which Fireman Rollin Morgan was killed.

According to a story in the *Sunbury American* of Friday, July 7, 1899, the boys placed an obstruction on the tracks causing the Philadelphia and Reading freight to jump the rails. The locomotive went over an embankment, killing

Morgan who was in the cab and causing injury to Engineer John Gardner.

Coal and Iron Police arrested the boys on the evidence of several witnesses who saw the boys in the vicinity prior to the mishap.

Just a week later, on July 14, the *American* reported the arrest of half a dozen boys ranging in age from 14 to 16 for attempted train wrecking on the Philadelphia and Reading at the Herndon and Main Line Junction, one mile west of Shamokin.

Officials said the boys tampered with switches, which could have caused accidents to both passenger and freight trains.

Such vandalism wasn't restricted to Northumberland County. In the same article, the newspaper reported the arrest of an eight-year-old and two seven-year-old boys from Gilberton who attempted to wreck a P&R passenger train on the steep mountainside at Frackville.

In this case, the boys placed an iron brake, shoe and heel, on the high rail of a sharp curve which rounded a 300-foot precipice just moments before the train arrived. The obstruction was placed in such a manner that when the pony wheel struck it, it fell from the wheel, averting the accident. An estimated 100 passengers were aboard the train.

TRAIN-JUMPERS

The young have a tendency to consider themselves invincible and have a tendency to engage in acts of daring for thrills and to test their bravery.

Newspapers of the nineteenth century are filled with reports of serious injuries and death occurring when people attempted to hop on or off passing trains. In the summer of 1892, hordes of illegal riders were causing a problem for area police. An article in the *Shamokin Herald* of June 24, 1892 reveals what they did about it.

"Ever since the warm weather set in it has been the habit of a number of young men and boys to board a Newberry freight train, leaving Shamokin every evening, and travel on

Herndon station. (Courtesy of Larry Deklinski, Delado Photography; Northumberland County Historical Society; and Paul Thomas Studios.)

it as far as Sunbury, where they would alight and bathe in the river. In a few hours a freight train South would approach on which the swimmers would return home. Time and again the police effected arrests but the gang increased in numbers.

"The officers held a consultation as to a plan leading to the successful capture of a majority of the riders. When the train left for Newberry last evening Officer James Lippiatt was on one end of the train and Henry Shovelin on the other. The crew was cautioned to secrecy. Hardly had the freight started until the midnight bathers, one by one, boarded the cars until about thirty-seven were safely on the moving train, whose speed grew more rapid until a rate of thirty miles an hour was obtained."

As the train passed Reed's Station, the officers closed in. Someone shouted "police," and a panic ensued. As the police took boys into custody, the more venturesome jumped off the train.

Thirteen boys were captured. They were identified as George Katerman, Joseph Clark, Albert Homer, Charles Rubright, Anthony Dick, Aleck Stricker, Harry Dezell, Edward Boyle, Charles Bashore, Charles Linderman, William Smith, William Long, and William Williams. They were taken before a magistrate and fined $3 each.

"About twenty-three of their companions escaped but the police have their names and by night the majority will have received a hearing, as their names are in possession of the officers.

"The habit of illegal car riding is indulged in extensively on the three roads running into town and the police should use every effort to break it up. There is too much danger in jumping on cars and a close observer would be astonished to find boys hardly able to walk indulging in the perilous practice."

Did the raids succeed in breaking up the perilous practice? Of course not. Boys will be boys.

NOT A NEW PROBLEM

A pair of serious accidents within days of one another prompted the *Shamokin Times* to issue a warning to boys in its Dec. 5, 1879 edition about the danger of taking trains for granted.

The newspaper reported that Weimar Snyder, about 14, a son of Harmon Snyder, had jumped on a coal train on Saturday, Nov. 29, to hitch a ride to Big Mountain colliery where he was employed.

"At Big Mountain the boy attempted to jump off the train and was thrown under the wheels of one of the cars, the wheels passing over his left leg and crushing the limb in a frightful manner."

The boy was taken to the residence of his parents on Commerce street, where his limb was amputated by Doctors E. S. Robins, C. W. Weaver, and M. H. Harpel.

The paper also reported that on Sunday, Nov. 30, ". . . Willie Long, son of Nicholas Long, started from home to go to Sunday School, and on his way, he climbed up on top of some house cars that were standing on the siding at the

Northern Central depot, and started to run along over the tops of the cars. Two of the cars were not coupled and were separated so far that the boy could not jump across the intervening space, and as a consequence he fell to the ground and had his forehead and nose badly cut, and also had his one leg fractured. He was carried home by Mr. H. H. Keiser, and Dr. Harpel was sent for, who dressed the boy's injuries."

These two accidents were coupled in one column with reports of Joseph Calvich of Springfield being injured by a fall of coal at the Cameron and John Edmunds of Dewart street fracturing three ribs in a fall from a battery at Buck Ridge colliery.

Apparently the newspaper considered these last two of such common occurrence they required no further comment. As to the injuries to the boys, they warranted a separate notice on the same page:

> The accidents to Weimar Snyder and Willie Long are additional warnings to the boys not to jump on or off moving trains, and to keep away from the cars even when they are not moving.
>
> "Shamokin has many boys who are in the habit of jumping on moving trains and some of these boys have been repeatedly warned, but it is probable that they will heed nothing that may be said and will continue the dangerous practice of fooling around the railroad until they meet with an accident similar to those noted above.

THREE IN A WEEK

A Shamokin engineer was killed and several others hurt in the third railroad accident in a week near Snydertown, it was reported in the Friday, Jan. 24, 1890 edition of the *Sunbury American.*

The report said Engineer Clark Hoffman was killed, Fireman William Gensil suffered internal injuries and brakeman Jesse Startzel was bruised about the face and body and had a finger smashed. All three were Shamokin residents.

"The wreck took place fifty yards west from the scene of the wreck on the previous Tuesday in which Conductor

Snydertown station. (Courtesy of Larry Deklinski, Delado Photography; Northumberland County Historical Society; and Paul Thomas Studios.)

Diefenderfer of Tamaqua was killed. The day following that wreck, three box cars went to smash on exactly the same spot caused by the spreading of rails."

The newspaper said the most recent accident involved a Reading train of 40 box and gondolas loaded with merchandise and coal, southbound from Newberry. "Engine No. 886 was in front and engine No. 859 was in the middle. The train was conducted by Martin Reppard, of Shamokin. It was very dark as the train thundered along the road at twenty miles an hour."

As the train neared Snydertown, the Shamokin Creek, skirted by a high embankment, was on the east side and there was a steep hill studded with large boulders on the southwest.

Suddenly, the engineer saw a large rock in the middle of the tracks. "He shut off steam and shouted a warning to Gensil and Reppard who were on the fireman's side of the cab, and before the men could recover from the confusion the wild cry produced, the engine plunged into the rock, weighing ten tons."

The cab raised in the air, turned completely around, and fell against three large spruce trees on the creek side. One of the trees sliced through the cab and struck the engineer. Gensil and Reppard were thrown out of the cab. Jesse Startzel, who was riding in the second car, was also hurled through the air.

The body of Hoffman was recovered from the engine which had rolled down the embankment and was lodged against a tree.

When a wreck train arrived later from Milton it was learned it had struck and killed an elderly man named William Blake several miles down the road. Blake, a peddler from Arters, had been walking on the track and was run down on a curve.

HEROIC FIREMAN

It's a given that the men who mined coal were a tough and resourceful lot. The same qualities apply to the railroaders who carried the coal to market.

Early newspapers frequently carried stories of railroaders who risked their own lives to prevent collisions. Here's an example from the March 21, 1890 edition of the *Shamokin Herald*:

"Fireman Peter Henninger, of the Reading road, had his nose and jaws badly injured in a fall from a bumper last night while engaged in saving his engineer, Lewy Boshler, and the crew from a probable frightful ending."

The incident occurred as the southbound train No. 43 went onto the bridge across the Susquehanna at Sunbury. It was a dark and foggy night and the train of numerous coal cars slowed as it crossed the river.

"When the last car stood on the centre of the bridge second section 873, made up of forty-five cars, came howling down the grade and on the bridge.

"The air brakes were applied as is always the case in crossing the river. The momentum of the train, however, was such that the steam did not have much effect on the appliances. On the train swept, when suddenly the glare of the headlight revealed to the startled eyes of Boshler and Henninger the rear end of the first section twenty-five yards ahead.

"The only salvation was to get the train stopped, as there was no possible way of escape, for a plunge into the dark waters below meant death by drowning and a collision would result in those horrible and numerous wrecks only known to happen on railroad bridges. The crew on the first section were unconscious of danger as were the brakemen of the latter, until the loud whistle of down brakes broke the quiet, when Boshler reversed."

It was then Henninger seized a torch, leapt over the tender, and landed by a brake, which he hurriedly set. He continued across the cars, setting three more brakes in succession.

"How he got over so many without falling between them is a mystery but at last the panting man stumbled and fell. As his body shot between two cars he threw out his hands and grasped the platform of a car. If he let go he would either be cut in half or fall in the river, and as he hung there, the man expected the crash to come and be mangled. It was a thrilling moment but by a superhuman effort he drew himself up and fell fainting on the coal as the train came to a stop."

RUNNING LATE

Heavy traffic, tight schedules, and faulty signals were among causes of the many accidents involving trains in the nineteenth and early twentieth centuries.

A Hazleton train running late may have been to blame for its collision with another North Central passenger train from Shamokin on Monday, Oct. 1, 1894, injuring eight people and causing several thousand dollars in damage.

"The Northern Central train from Shamokin was coming around the horn north of the Pennsylvania station and was just crossing what is locally known as the straight track when the train from Hazleton was approaching," the *Sunbury Evening Item* reported, "and before a stop could be made it crashed into the smoking car of the Shamokin train, striking broadside. The side was smashed in and the car thrown over on its side."

Both trains carried a full capacity of passengers. Fortunately, only eight were injured. They were:

C. G. Murphy, Centralia, associate judge of Columbia County, scalp wound; A. W. Calhoun, Sunbury, a Western Union lineman, left wrist cut and left leg badly bruised; James H. Brownell, Centralia, scalp wound; Charles Charlton, Philadelphia, head and hand cuts; Walter F. Hurcame, Huntingdon, scalp wound; Elmer Hess, Shamokin, scalp wound; Theodore Teats, Harrisburg, back, leg and facial injuries; Abraham Persing, Sunbury, hand injury.

Though none of the injuries were deemed serious, the newspaper stressed it was a narrow escape for passengers in the upset smoker car. "The side that was struck by the Hazleton engine was completely smashed to splinters, the seats broken and tumbled in confusion, and the lamps shattered into a thousand fragments."

The reporter added, "The engineer of the Shamokin train was William (Tommy) Umplebe and Thomas Attick engineer of the other. Both had signals to come in and neither saw the other coming in time to avert the collision, although they both had brought the speed of their trains down before they struck. Had they come together running at their usual speed at that point a number of horrible deaths would surely have been the result."

No Serious Injuries

The collision of a freight train from Mount Carmel and a Wilkes-Barre passenger train caused considerable damage but no serious injuries on Jan. 12, 1894 in Sunbury.

A story in the Jan. 13 edition of the *Evening Item* attributed the accident to speed and an apparent misreading of signals by the Wilkes-Barre crew. The report noted the freight train was running about seven hours late and had stopped because it was time for the passenger train north.

"The train for Wilkes-Barre is the last one to leave the station on the North and West Branch Road, and follows Fast Line very closely. After Fast Line went north, the switchman signaled Engineer Harvey Brumbach, who was running the fast freight to come into the DY yard, and he of course obeyed the signal and started his train.

"After crossing what is known as the new track with his engine and part of his train the Wilkes-Barre passenger train, in charge of Engineer John Moyer and Conductor Zach Moyer, came thundering up the new track and struck the freight broadside, ploughing through it and scattering cars and merchandise in every direction."

Despite the impact, the passenger train didn't leave the tracks and the engine had only minor damage. But the freight was badly wrecked with six cars being thrown down the embankment, two on the east side and four on the west side of the track.

The car struck by the locomotive was split in half and the contents—which included upright pianos, wallpaper, and a quantity of hats—were scattered a considerable distance along the tracks.

John Teats, express messenger, and James Law, baggage master, suffered minor injuries. Some passengers were shaken, but none were injured.

When the crash occurred, Teats was in the act of moving a crate of chickens from one side of the car to the other. He was thrown down, and the chicken coop landed on top of him. He said had the express matter and baggage been loaded on the opposite side of the car from where it was all hands in the car would have been killed or seriously injured.

One passenger on the train commented he was getting used to accidents since this was the second wreck he had been in that day.

A TERRIBLE MISTAKE

As many as 11 persons from the Shamokin-Mount Carmel area were believed to be among 13 killed in a head-on collision of two passenger trains of the Lehigh Valley Railroad on Jan. 9, 1899 near West Dunellen, N.J.

A story in the Jan. 10 edition of the *Evening Item*, Sunbury, reported more than 25 persons were seriously injured in the spectacular accident which resulted, first, from a "terrible mistake" in train orders and, second, due to another accident on the same line earlier in the day.

The area victims were identified as Martin Keenan, hotel keeper, Mount Carmel; W. H. Hinkle, contractor, Mount Carmel; Jacob Heller, 40, tailor, Mount Carmel; H. E. Weikell, 25, Mount Carmel; Frank Fischer, 28, shoe dealer, Mount Carmel; William H. Leader, 24, dry goods dealer, Mount Carmel, son of C. C. Leader, a Shamokin bank president; Frank Markel, 54, Shamokin; Theodore Steckla, Shamokin; Abner S. Keifer, carpet dealer, Pottsville; William H. Markel, Shamokin, and James Jarvis, 12, Mount Carmel.

Follow up stories in the *Shamokin Daily Dispatch* listed seven fatalities, identifying them as Warren H. Merkel, Rufus and H. E. Weikel, George Joseph, William C. Leader, May Sminkey, and Theodore Steckla.

A number of other area residents were among the injured. These included Nicholas, Henry, Louis and Mary Parecca, all of Shamokin; Joseph Malesky, Shenandoah; Mary Jarville, Mount Carmel; George Launesky, Mount Carmel; Harry R. Foster, Pottsville; Miss Annie Jones, Shamokin; L. B. Wachter, Mount Carmel; William Feely, Pottsville, and Abraham Allgier, Mount Carmel.

Among its dispatches from the scene, the Associated Press reported a "miracle." The four-month-old child of the Pareccas, mentioned as among the injured, flung out of the mother's arms, was found alive among the wreckage, and suffered only minor bruises.

Mrs. Parreca told a reporter, "I was nursing the baby, when the whistle began to blow. My husband started to open the window. Then I was thrown to the back of the car and lost consciousness. My baby was gone."

The mother said she was frantic until it was discovered her baby had been found by rescue crews and was safe.

The earlier accident occurred when the axle of a freight car broke, causing a pile up which blocked eastbound tracks. Throughout the morning, Lehigh Valley trains bound for New York were switched to the west, then around to another line headed toward their destination. As a precaution, other westbound traffic was held at South Plainfield, N.J. until the line was clear of trains going in the opposite direction.

Train No. 20, which left Shamokin at seven that morning, was so heavily laden with passengers it had to be broken into three sections. The first two sections arrived at Bound Brook, switched over to the other track, then switched back at Newmarket and reached New York in safety. The third section, part of a three-day businessmen's excursion to New York and crowded with some 400 passengers, was running about an hour late.

Somewhere near Dunellen, a signal man miscued and allowed a westbound train to proceed. The local put on steam and headed round a curve, going about 25 miles an hour. In the cab of the excursion train, the engineer and fireman saw the approaching local. Frantically, they applied brakes and whistles.

But it was too late.

Crews of both engines jumped before the pilotless engines collided, the local turning a complete somersault before tipping and the lead car of the excursion train rolling over. Both engines were demolished, but it was the first car of the excursion train in which the majority of the deaths and serious injuries occurred. The other cars, though their passengers were badly shaken, remained on the tracks.

STALLED BY A BLIZZARD

A blizzard, with drifts up to 30-feet in height in some places, put a stop to railroad traffic in the coal regions in February 1899, but, fortunately, no serious injuries were reported.

The *Evening Herald*, Shenandoah, reported on Monday, Feb. 13., the town was completely cut off from traffic with other communities and many trains were snowbound as heavy snow continued to fall and "immense drifts and great gales" left local business paralyzed. Collieries were at a standstill and schools were closed. It was anticipated the blizzard might last another day or two.

"All the railroads are more or less demoralized by the blizzard and it is with the greatest difficulty that any service at all is kept up with the outside districts," the *Herald* said.

The only serious injury reported on the line was that of David Houser, 60, an engineer from Mount Carmel. He was

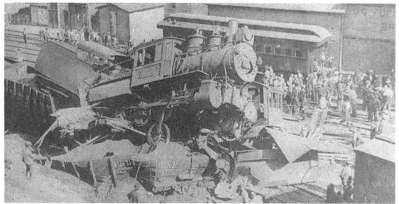

Reading crash. (Courtesy of Louis Polyniak Collection.)

standing on the tank of one engine near Mahanoy City when a second was brought up and coupled. A coupling broke and the sudden movement threw Houser between the tank and near engine. He was dragged some distance before his cries were heard and the engine stopped. His forehead was gashed, he was bruised about the body and his left leg was scalded by steam.

Rail contact with Shenandoah was re-established on Feb. 15.

"Affairs were in such a deplorable condition yesterday that none of the railroad companies were disposed to count upon a re-establishment of any kind within twenty-four hours, but they accomplished much better work than was estimated.

"Traffic is again established between this town and Pottsville on both the P&R and Pennsylvania railroads, and the former also has its line from Ashland to Mahanoy Plane open."

The Lehigh Valley was still struggling to open its branches. But the newspaper did say an engine with one passenger coach ran from Delano to Shenandoah and from there to Mount Carmel late the previous night.

Among snowbound cars of the Catawissa branch of the P&R was one loaded with western horses and another with cattle. Some of the animals had died from exposure and lack of water.

The storm put a heavy expense on the railroads. One report said the Shamokin Division of the P&R employed 2,500 extra men to shovel snow from the tracks.

NARROW ESCAPE

Harry Miller, a clerk at the DL&W depot in Danville, narrowly escaped death in a yard accident, the *Danville Intelligencer* reported on July 29, 1904

"It is part of Harry's duty to take the number of all freight cars entering the Danville yard. He walked up the track from the depot to the 'Nail Mill Switch' on Saturday morning to take the numbers of several cars that the Danville engine was about to push into a siding north of the main track.

"The engine was pushing the cars intended for this switch, and was also pulling another to be run on the siding south of the main track. Harry did not see this car and had stepped on the south side switch to get out of the way of the train."

The train had picked up speed and as the rear car rolled into the siding, it struck the clerk.

"He fell full length, the front truck missing him completely. The rear truck, however, caught his clothing and dragged him quite a distance. The brakes were set on the car and it came to a stop shortly after it entered or the result would have been far more serious."

Miller escaped with bruises to his face and body and a "bad" fright.

PASSENGERS FRIGHTENED

There were no injuries, but passengers aboard a Reading train received a scare in an accident that occurred in January 1906 near Arters Station.

The *Danville Intelligencer* of Jan. 19 reported, "While the train was running along at a rapid rate of speed the cylinder head on one side of the engine blew out and striking the passenger coach tore a large hole in the side of the car."

The passengers were bound from Sunbury to Shamokin.

"After running about a half mile the train was brought to a standstill and when the extent of the damage was learned the car was cut from the train and the passengers were transferred to the Pullman car," the *Intelligencer* said. "When the train arrived at Shamokin another engine and passenger coach was received and the train proceeded for Philadelphia about one hour and a half late."

KILLED ON BRIDGE

Two people were killed on Sunday, Jan. 21, 1906 when they were struck by an engine while walking across the Pennsylvania railroad bridge at Selinsgrove.

The victims were identified as Miss Mary Cornwall, 23, of Sunbury and formerly of Danville, and Murray Heider, 15, Selinsgrove, in a report on Jan. 26 in the *Danville Intelligencer*.

The report said Miss Cornwall had been visiting Miss Bertha Jarrett in Selinsgrove and was to return home on the evening of the accident.

"As no passenger trains are run by the way of Selinsgrove on Sundays it was necessary to walk across the railroad bridge in order to catch the train for Sunbury at Selinsgrove Junction. Accordingly Miss Cornwall and Miss Jarrett accompanied by Murray Heider and Cleveland Kratzer, of Selinsgrove, started to walk to Selinsgrove Junction."

They were nearly at the last span of the bridge when they heard a train coming behind them. Miss Jarrett and Kratzer stepped off the bridge onto a pier where they would be safe. Apparently believing they could outrun the train, the two victims started off at a faster pace. The *Intelligencer* said they ". . . had just about reached the middle of the span when an engine, car and caboose came bearing down upon them running at the rate of fifteen miles an hour."

A DEADLY DREAM

Mrs. Fred Fitch of Canal street, Schuylkill Haven, dreamed one night her husband, a flagman on the Reading, had been killed in a railroad accident. Worried, she told Fred about her dream and urged him to be careful when he next went to work.

Mrs. Fitch—Minnie E. nee Miller—a niece of Margaret E. (Becker) Lindermuth, my great-grandmother, was subsequently informed by a Reading crew caller that Fred had, indeed, been killed in an accident on Nov. 11, 1917.

Fred had been on the crew of Engine No. 1736 which had taken eighty-two loaded coal cars down the main line. M. L. Smith, also of Schuylkill Haven, was engineer and a man named Leddy of St. Clair was the conductor.

The Call reported, in part, on Nov. 17:

> Fitch was a flagman and was alone in the caboose at the time of the accident. His lifeless remains were discovered by the members of a northbound coal train crew but a few minutes following the accident. This crew in turn notified his own crew and that was the first knowledge of the accident.

It was believed Fred had alighted from the caboose to get a drink and when cars came together he was knocked down and fell under the wheels of the cars. In addition to his wife, he was survived by two daughters, Mildred and Laverne, and his mother, Sarah Jane (Sowers) Krammer.

6

LABOR WOES

BROTHERHOOD OF THE FOOTBOARD

Like most workers in the early nineteenth century, railroaders had no job security. There were no such things as seniority rights, safety laws, or insurance to provide for them and their families in the event of injury.

There were no unions to protect them prior to 1863 and most private companies would not sell insurance to railroad workers because of the dangers of the job.

Complain about pay and discuss forming a union and you'd likely be fired. This was at a time when the average pay amounted to a dollar a day and, statistically, most workers could expect to suffer injury of some kind while on the job.

Train crews were often on call around the clock, disrupting family life and contributing to the possibility a man might fall prey to such vices as drinking and gambling.

It was such concerns that led to the formation of the Brotherhood of the Footboard on May 8, 1863 at Marshall, Mich., the first union for railroad workers in the United States. This was the forerunner of the Brotherhood of Locomotive Engineers and Trainmen to which most of my railroading ancestors belonged.

The first tussle of the Brotherhood of the Footboard with a railroad company came in July 1864 when employees of the Philadelphia and Reading went on strike for better wages. Unfortunately, the union wasn't yet strong enough and the company retaliated by laying off the strikers.

Slowly the union built up its strength, changed its name to the Brotherhood of Locomotive Engineers, became better organized, and began chipping away at the leviathans with which it tangled.

Following the Civil War, most railroad companies followed the lead of mining and other businesses and consolidated into huge corporations which put their emphasis on profit over all other concerns. Conditions, obviously, worsened for the worker whose demands for wage increases and complaints proved an irritation rather than a matter to be addressed.

THE STRIKE OF 1877

The first national strike broke out in 1877 and was a bloody one. The nation was in a depression, the longest and toughest in U.S. history until that time. It lasted an astonishing 65 months. During that period, thousands of businesses went bankrupt, unemployment soared, and the economy stalled.

An article in the July 12, 1877 edition of the *Carbon Advocate*, Lehighton, commented on the situation in the vicinity of Mauch Chunk:

> The men, reduced to a mere pittance, look sad and dejected;
> merchants carry small stocks and, though the majority
> of them are still doing business on the ruinous credit
> system, customers appear to be wanting even at that, a fact
> that would seem to indicate a very general disposition to
> economize.

In response to the crisis, stronger companies such as the railroads which had been enjoying a boom prior to the downturn sought to cut expenses in any way possible. They laid off workers and, in some cases, replaced them with new immigrants willing to work for less pay. They also reduced wages all along the line. Reaction came when they sought to impose another 10 percent cut less than a year after the first. The Pennsy anticipated saving a million and a half dollars with a planned 10 percent reduction in employee wages.

Remember that the Reading, under its president Franklin B. Gowen, was heavily invested in coal lands and mining,

Reading massacre contemporary newspaper illustration.

a factor that made it especially vulnerable. The company had been dealing with strikes by miners since the beginning of the decade and now rail crews were threatening to go out. Unable to borrow at home or abroad, the Reading and others involved in mining were obliged to sell their coal at prices it could command in a badly deflated market.

Gowen, who had destroyed the Workmens' Benevolent Association, an early attempt at unionization, was now a celebrity as a result of his brutal crackdown on the Molly Maguires, an alleged Irish terrorist organization he blamed for all the labor agitation. Twenty accused Mollies were hanged, primarily on the evidence of James McParland, a Pinkerton detective hired by Gowen to infiltrate the ranks of the organization.

The railroad strike broke out on July 14, 1877 in Martinsburg, West Virginia, and quickly spread to Maryland, Pennsylvania, New York, and then west to Illinois and Missouri.

Ironically, Gowen had just returned from a European vacation and one of his first acts was to sign an order calling for reducing the number of brakemen on passenger trains.

Among the scenes of violence in Pennsylvania was Reading, namesake of the railroad. Some 1,500 men in the community were employed by the railroad and public sentiment was with them.

Saturday, July 21, was payday and, to their surprise, the railroad men were paid. Later that day it was learned 150 machinists had been furloughed. This and news of events in West Virginia and at Pittsburgh spurred hot tempers and brought threats of possible property damage. It was reported militia had fired on strikers in Pittsburgh and people had been injured. In fact, 10 persons had been killed in Pittsburgh where the strike was against the Pennsylvania Railroad Company.

All across the state, militias had been put on alert. Company A, Fourth Regiment (Reading Rifles) of the Pennsylvania National Guard was called to assembly at Fourth and Penn's Square. Some refused to muster, not wanting to fight men whose lot was little different than their own and who might even be relatives. Those who did gather were mocked and insulted.

When nothing had happened by nightfall, the soldiers disbanded and went home.

That evening, representatives of the Brotherhood of Locomotive Engineers met to discuss whether to remain on strike. Alan Pinkerton, whose detective agency had been hired by Gowen to boost his coal and iron police force, accused the union of having met that night to plan destructive acts that occurred later.

In the wake of growing, angry crowds by Monday, there came incidents of arson, beatings of ambushed soldiers and men sympathetic to the railroad, and, finally, stoppage of a freight train. No trains were to get through in the coming hours.

A supplement of some 300 men from the Fourth Pennsylvania Volunteer Militia, commanded by General Franklin Reeder, arrived to back up local police, coal and iron officers, Pinkerton's detectives, and the Reading Rifles, most of whom had decamped by that time. The contingent of 14 Coal and Iron Police was under command of Captain James Alderson of Shamokin.

When this force clashed with the strikers and their allies, including women who threw stones at the soldiers, shots rang out. When the smoke cleared, 16 citizens lay dead on the streets of Reading.

A Corporal Kendall, a member of the Reading Rifles, was found guilty in a court-martial at Harrisburg and dishonorably discharged for allegedly joining the mob and stoning his fellow troopers. The military then turned him over to civil authorities for further action.

On July 23, in Sunbury, seat of Northumberland County, railroad workers assisted by other citizens began stopping trains. In Danville, Montour County, on the same day workers demanded the borough provide either work or bread. When neither was forthcoming, groups began foraging for weapons. They clashed with police, but no shots were fired. After a conference, the borough began distributing food to those in need.

On July 25, in Shamokin, an estimated 1,000 men, many of them coal miners, united with the railroaders in seeking better working conditions, stormed the Reading's depot, and clashed with police and a militia led by Mayor William Douty.

In the exchange of shots, innocent bystanders were struck down. Reporting on what followed the first volley, the *Carbon Advocate* said:

"The scene which followed was terrible. The police mortally wounded a man named Wiest, a storekeeper, and injured several others, among them Robert Thompson and a lad named Shoops, who were among the spectators. The latter who was shot in the head, will not survive. After the first shooting the citizens held a meeting in the Presbyterian church and after they had gotten through with it they found that several buildings had been fired."

Wiest, who operated a candy store at Liberty and Independence streets, succumbed to his wound. Levi Shoop also died. Twelve or 14 others were injured in the shootings.

In the fall term of court in Northumberland County five men were given jail terms for their actions in the Shamokin riot. They were Philip Weist, Christian Neely, Peter Campbell, James Richards, and James Ebright.

Business was at the standstill for a week at Shenandoah where up to a thousand men paraded with flags and a drum corps while stables were torched at nearby Lost Creek.

On July 28 the *Carbon Advocate* reported all quiet in some of the hotbeds and said trains were resuming runs on several lines. The correspondent commented:

> Mauch Chunk, always quiet and orderly, is decidedly so now; in fact it is almost too quiet for endurance. But this may only be the calm before the storm, and it would be useless to deny that considerable uneasiness exists in the community at large with regard to the future. On the whole, however, all classes are agreed in this that, happen what will, they will see to it that order is maintained in the town.

He noted that, as a precaution, the brass cannon at the rear of the courthouse had been moved to the town arsenal—the county jail.

By the time it was all over, The Great Strike had a final toll of a hundred people killed and more than 1,000 serving jail terms of various lengths. Though it was questionable how much the strikers gained, the walkout did make it clear laborers would no longer tolerate corporate oppression and would mobilize to demand fairer treatment.

Yet, as late as 1882 when un-unionized freight handlers in New York went on strike, seeking a pay raise of from 17 to 20 cents an hour, strike breakers were called in and the walkout quashed.

UNION CONVENTION

> NEW YORK, Feb. 1 (1892)—The Railway Employees of America held their annual convention at the Academy of Music here yesterday. About two thousand delegates representing the Brotherhoods of Locomotive Engineers, Conductors, of Railway Trainmen, of Railway Firemen, and the Order of Railway Telegraphers. Sessions were held both in the morning and afternoon. The deliberations were secret.

THE PULLMAN STRIKE

The next big test for unions would be the Pullman Strike of 1894.

Again it came on the heels of a financial panic. Some 16,000 U.S. businesses had failed in 1893 and thousands more faced bankruptcy by the spring of 1894. As before, businesses sought to reduce costs and maintain capital. As before, railroads were once again slashing payrolls and furloughing men.

Wage cuts and layoffs fell full force on the Chicago suburb of Pullman, where the Pullman Palace Car Company was both the sole employer and landlord.

George M. Pullman behaved like a feudal landlord, exercising even more control over the lives of his employees and their families than the worst of the coal barons. He'd banned saloons and the eight-hour day along with trade unions. He had spies everywhere and all the employees knew they could be fired anytime at his whim.

Conditions became even more severe as Pullman tightened the economic reins. Believing they had little to lose, a majority of the employees joined the American Railway Union, founded by Eugene V. Debs.

At noon on May 11, they walked out on strike.

The *Evening Herald,* Shenandoah, reported on May 12, 1894:

> Two thousand employees of the Pullman Palace Car Company quit work yesterday. Those who went out asserted that the entire force of 4,300 persons would join the strike.
>
> Trouble has been brewing for some time, the men demanding the restoration of a 33 1/2 per cent cut in their wages made last year. The employers refused the demand and asserted that they were running the plant for the purpose of giving the men employment.

On the same date, the *Scranton Tribune* reported the number of strikers at between 2,000 and 3,000.

Their action took Pullman and his active manager by
surprise, as it was understood that the men were satisfied
with the result of the recent conference.

Employing all the many skills to hand, Debs orated,
seeking support for the workers; parleyed with anyone he
thought might help win an advantage, and frequently visited
the town of Pullman to confer and listen to the complaints
of its inhabitants. Wanting a peaceful settlement, he urged
against violence.

When Pullman declined to bend, the union delivered an
ultimatum giving the company five days in which to begin
arbitration or face a boycott in which railroad workers would
refuse to move any train attached to a Pullman car.

Switchmen were the first to act, refusing to attach Pullman's cars to trains they handled. Within days, all traffic
west of Chicago was halted. Though railroad men in the east
sympathized with the Pullman workers, they faced their own
problems and declined to give physical support to the strike.

In a report on the Pullman boycott on June 27 the *Evening Herald* said:

President Debs asks the co-operation of the Brotherhood
of Railway Trainmen. The officers of that body manifest a
disposition not to be drawn into the trouble, asserting that
they had nothing to do with the strike at Pullman or its
consequences.

Responding to charges the stoppages were delaying
mail—a violation of the Sherman Anti-Trust Act—President
Grover Cleveland sent in federal troops on July 3 to squash
the strike.

There was some resistance from strikers, the burning of
some dozen freight cars, the overturning of some coaches of
the troop train, and disabling of its engine, but it wasn't long
before trains were running in all directions and on schedule.
The railroads stated they would consider no compromise
and those who did not return to work were assured they
would be replaced.

The *Herald* of July 5 reported:

HARPER'S WEEKLY

> There is absolutely no obstruction to the movements of the mails east of Chicago. All the lines between Chicago and St. Paul are now open, and as far west as Cheyenne the road is clear. There is no accumulation of mail matter anywhere except at points in the far west.

Cover cartoon by W. A. Rogers for Harpers Weekly, July 14, 1894.

Debs and a number of union officers were arrested, arraigned on charges of conspiracy to halt the movement of the mail, accusations which sent the union leader to jail for six months.

The strike was again a loss for the workers, but sympathy for them did boost public sentiment in favor of unions.

LABOR DAY

Perhaps in regret for the bloodshed at the hands of troops during the Pullman strike, President Grover Cleveland sought to reconcile with the labor movement. Congress unanimously approved Labor Day as a national holiday and Cleveland signed it into law just six days after the end of the strike in 1894.

The idea for a day to celebrate labor originated with unionists as early as the 1880s and it was observed annually in several states before Cleveland made it a national holiday. The first Monday in September was selected as an alternative to May 1, the original choice of the labor movement. Cleveland feared May 1, observed as International Workers' Day, would encourage socialist and anarchist groups and might spur more events like the bloody Haymarket Affair of 1886.

THE ERDMAN ACT

A major victory for the unions was the passage of the Erdman Act of 1898.

Sponsored by Constantine Jacob Erdman, a Pennsylvania Democrat and member of the U.S. House, the act set up an arbitration and collective bargaining process, protected the right of workers to belong to a union,

Constantine Jacob Erdman (Bio photo from Directory of U.S. Congress.)

and made it illegal for companies to fire a worker during the arbitration process, unless there was sufficient evidence of neglect of duties.

In 1908, by a six-two vote, the Supreme Court determined the section of the act making it illegal to fire an employee for belonging to a union was unconstitutional. The Erdman Act was a predecessor to the more comprehensive Railway Labor Act of 1926.

Still, it was, perhaps, Erdman's most significant achievement as a Congressman and it gained him a national reputation. It's interesting to note Erdman was one of those troops called to duty in 1877 to put down rioters. He had his collarbone broken during the riots in Reading where he served as adjutant of the Fourth Regiment, Pennsylvania National Guard.

WAGES, UP AND DOWN

Wages were among issues to remain a concern in coming years.

In the spring of 1904, the Brotherhood of Railway Trainmen demanded a revision of the wage scale for trainmen on the Pennsylvania lines, contending they were not paid as much as those on lines west of Chicago.

The *Sunbury American* said:

The trainmen are asking for 30 and 28 cents per hour
for yard brakemen, 31 and 33 cents per hour for yard
conductors, and pay by the mile instead of the day for road
trainmen.

WORK SUSPENSION

This article from the Friday, June 17, 1904 *Danville Intelligencer* illustrates the concerns of workmen in that year:

"Some of the departments at the Pennsylvania railroad
shops presented a deserted appearance Wednesday, owing
to the retrenchment order received on Tuesday.

"In the blacksmith, machine and boiler departments
there was no one working except the foremen of the departments. The employees will work five hours on Thursday and
then again remain idle on Friday. Just how long this order of working will continue has not been determined. The
order has reduced wages to such an extent that many of
the employees will be unable to meet their necessary living
expenses.

"Four hundred employees were suspended at Altoona,
making the total 2,700 at that place now idle. (Copied from
Sunbury Item)"

SHOP WORKERS STRIKE

The Railroad Labor Board announced in 1922 wages for
shop workers would be cut by seven percent. In early July,
some 400,000 railroad shop laborers went on strike. Railroads retaliated by replacing strikers with non-union men.
As the strike dragged on a federal judge imposed a ban on
all strike-related activities. The unions finally settled in October for a five percent wage cut.

FEDERAL ACTS

Railroading may have faded away, but labor and the need for unions remains a matter of concern for most workers.

A number of federal acts improved the welfare of railroad workers late in the nineteenth and early in the twentieth centuries. In 1908, the Federal Employers' Liability Act made for a 10-hour work day and in 1911, the Brotherhoods won an eight-hour day. The railroads weren't consistent in abiding by the eight-hour rule.

Faced with the threat of another nationwide strike, Congress passed the Adamson Act in 1916, stipulating the work day as eight hours for all interstate railroad employees.

The U.S. Railroad Labor Board was created in 1920 and authorized to intercede in disputes between the companies and their employees. This boards' effectiveness was undermined by the fact compliance with its decisions was not obligatory. That weakness was overcome in 1926 with passage of the Railway Labor Act which set in place stricter rules for collective bargaining, arbitration, and other matters.

Gains and losses continued in coming decades until the formation of Conrail. What happened after that is another story.

7

INNOVATIONS

The early railroad was seen as the greatest technological achievement of its time. It was big business defined, employing legions of men (and even some women), providing cheap transportation over longer distances—even uniting the country, east to west and north to south. In addition to these obvious factors of importance to the economy, it inspired ingenious men to invent means of making it more efficient, more profitable, and more valuable to everyone.

Some of these inventions made the job easier on the rail workers. Others were geared to the comfort and convenience of the public.

THE HEADLIGHT

Obviously, for maximum profit, it was necessary for railroads to operate both day and night. One might imagine the headlight was invented in order for the engineer to see where he was going. Since trains run on a defined plane, that is, the track, the engineer's need to see is of secondary importance. The more important need of a light was to provide warning of its approach to anyone walking or crossing the tracks.

The earliest trains might have been lighted by means of open fires built atop the engine. Whale oil provided illumination or reflective lamps until kerosene became available circa 1859.

Kerosene (manufactured from the oil first discovered at Titusville, Pennsylvania) provided a more intense light and was cheaper, at about 60 cents a gallon, than whale oil, which had risen in price to over a dollar a gallon in part due to the depletion of the whale population.

Kerosene remained the primary fuel until Thomas Edison provided the means for an electrical source. The only competition for his incandescent lamp was the arc lamp invented by Charles Francis Brush (patents 1878-1885). Others would tinker and make improvements in coming years.

4-4-0

Henry Roe Campbell of Philadelphia patented the first 4-4-0 locomotive on Feb. 6, 1837. Also known as the eight-wheel or American Type, it became, with some modifications, the most popular type of engine in the U.S. into the 1890s.

The numbers signify the arrangement of four leading wheels on two axles.

The initial design outperformed the strongest of the 4-2-0 engines built by Baldwin. But the rigidity of the American's frame and driving gear made it subject to frequent derailment. Additional patents by Campbell and work by others eventually eliminated or lessened the problem.

The 4-4-0 was among a number of contributions Campbell made to railroading. He laid out routes for several lines, built railroad bridges, and served as chief engineer for railroads in Pennsylvania and Vermont. He was also the engineer for construction of the freight yard and shop at Renovo in 1866.

IMPROVED ENGINE

Evening Herald, Jan. 5, 1899

"The Pennsylvania Railroad Company has placed an improved engine on the Pottsville short line to this town. The engine is a large one and similar to those in use on the main lines. The improvement consists of brakes connected with the pony truck under the front part of the engine, insuring additional security on heavy grades and affording additional facilities for rapid stops. The engine is also equipped with chime whistle."

TRAIN WHISTLE

For those of us who grew up hearing them, there are few sounds more nostalgic than that of the steam locomotive.

Though I'm certain it had a more practical purpose such as warning man or beast as the train rounded the curve, my sister and I came to believe a story related to the whistle. We were told dad would have his engineer sound the horn as the freight passed near our home to signal mom to get ready to make supper as he'd soon be home. Trainmen did have a code of long and short whistles to communicate with one another.

There are many types of whistle but the three and five-chime were the most popular. The Reading Railroad was famous for the shrill six-chimers used on their passenger lines. That of the Reading's freights was more of a "hoot."

The Pennsy also had a distinctive sound.

Like the headlight, the whistle wasn't a toy but rather a safety device.

The invention of the steam whistle is credited to George Stephenson, a British engineer, in 1832. The popular chime whistle was an adaptation by the Nathan Company of New York. Whistles were made in this country by a number of commercial firms, though many were also made in the railroad shops.

The whistle is activated by the engineer pulling on a cord or lever which releases steam into the mechanism. Engineers soon learned to operate the system with a degree of individuality by manipulating volume and pitch.

Their blare soon gave rise to noise complaints. There's no denying they were loud and, considering how near some houses sat to railroad tracks, one can sympathize with the displeasure. A writer in the Sept. 7, 1888 issue of the *Shamokin Herald* complained of 'chime cranks.'

"I think it was an Englishman who is credited with having given the name of 'American Devils' to steam whistles, a very appropriate appellation for the article of which Shamokin must certainly be the centre," he wrote. "Every locomotive that enters the town—the number is legion—gives vent to all the noise it contains."

THE TELEGRAPH

"What hath God Wrought?" This was the question asked in the first public message sent out over the telegraph system developed by Samuel Morse way back in 1843.

What had been wrought was a means of transmitting messages between separate points faster than any previously devised.

Morse, an artist prior to becoming an inventor, did not invent the telegraph. The concept can be traced back to such primitive predecessors as smoke signals and flashing mirrors. An actual machine can be traced to one Claude Chappe in France in the 1790s with more innovative stops along the way before we reach Morse.

What Morse did was develop the idea for sending a coded message (the dot and dash Morse code) over a single wire electric telegraph. Other inventors tinkered with the tool and submitted patents. By 1851 there were as many as 75 telegraph companies competing for a market share in the U.S.

Business was the primary customer, and a demanding one.

The telegraph proved its usefulness over and over again during the Mexican and Civil wars. By 1866 Western Union had achieved market dominance, beating out all competitors.

Railroads began using the telegraph in 1851 and operators soon demonstrated its advantages. Messages could be communicated between stations with immediacy and accuracy. Station masters could be kept aware of the location of every train under their responsibility at all times.

Railroads and new telegraph lines went west in tandem.

Alexander Graham Bell's invention of the telephone in 1876 might have stifled the usefulness of the telegraph for some businesses. The railroad wasn't among them. I remember visits to the telegrapher's office as a boy and seeing both a telephone and a telegraph sounder on his desk. The dispatcher phoned in his orders and the telegrapher clacked out his reports to the appropriate recipients, utilizing both instruments without giving one honor above the other.

In some places, telegraphers worked for both the railroad and Western Union, transmitting and receiving messages for the public on behalf of the latter, the additional money a welcome supplement to many, especially in the days before telegraphers got their own union.

From the *Danville Intelligencer*, June 17, 1904:

"Station Improvements"
The D.L.&W. Railroad Company has made new improvements in its office connected with the station here by installing all new telegraph instruments along with a new table to support them.

The improved equipment comprises one additional wire extending from Scranton to Sunbury. The new wire previously extended only as far as Berwick. Its extension to take in the entire division will facilitate communication considerably.

BLOCK SIGNAL SYSTEM

Because trains often ran in opposite directions on the same tracks, it was important for the trainmaster and crews to know the whereabouts of their counterparts. This need led to development of the timetable. We've also noted other methods by which rail workers communicated with one another—lights, whistles, flags, and the telegraph.

The speed of the telegraph aided greatly in notifying crews of timetable changes and new orders.

In the early days, men with flags were placed at specific locations to signal tracks were clear ahead or occupied. The fact that humans are capable of error and weather conditions may interfere with signals spurred the need for a better system and led to the development of fixed mechanical signals.

Railway lines were divided into sections known as blocks, each averaging from six to 10 miles in length. When a train entered a block, the signalman would set the lever to designate danger. When he received notice the track was clear, he would reset the lever to that status.

Ashbel Welch, a civil engineer, developed and installed the first block signaling system on the Camden and Amboy

Railroad's line between Philadelphia and New Brunswick, N.J., in 1863. It was ultimately adopted by all U.S. railroads, though with the usual delays.

An article in the Oct. 31, 1892 *Evening Herald* of Shenandoah announced the Reading company was adopting the block signal system on the line between Pottsville and Philadelphia.

Ashbel Welch
(Courtesy of Mazagine of Western History, *1888.)*

"By this system of automatic signaling the engineer of the train will always know whether the track for two blocks ahead is occupied or not, and as his locomotive passes over the point at which the signal's connection is made it will operate not only the signal ahead of him, but will also give notice two blocks in the rear."

The *Herald* explained the system worked by a combination of compressed air and electricity. "Pipes of an inch and a half to two inches in diameter will be laid alongside of the tracks and connected with the switches which can only be operated by train passing over the connections."

Welch was an early advocate for the use of telegraphy in railroad operations.

In a paper sent to a committee of the Franklin Institute of Philadelphia, Welch explained his signal used a white board, with a light showing through at night from a hole, in a black signal box, placed so it could be seen clearly from as far a distance as possible. A partition in the box separated signals for opposite directions.

"The signals are exhibited to the approaching train by the attendant at the telegraphic instrument pulling a cord or lever," Welch wrote, "and then the moment the engine passes letting it go, when the signal drops into the lower part of the box out of sight."

The signals were white for "clear" and red for "stop." After adoption by the Pennsylvania Railroad a third color, green, was added to permit temporary stoppages in long blocks.

AUTOMATIC COUPLER

An amateur inventor and store clerk was responsible for an invention that has saved the hands, limbs, and lives of countless railroaders since 1868.

Eli Hamilton Janney, a Virginian who had served with the Confederate Army in the Civil War, loved to tinker when business was slow in the store where he clerked near Alexandria, Va. During his military service and later, he'd become aware of the dangers railroaders incurred with the then-predominant link and pin system of coupling cars. It was necessary to step between cars to insert a pin or remove one from the link. If a car was bumped by another and shifted, the worker could be crushed between them.

As an example of this danger, 415 men were killed in 1891 and more than 9,000 injured in coupling cars.

Janney thought there must be a better way of coupling. He tinkered and came up with a prototype he patented in 1868. It didn't work. He tinkered more and came up with a new design similar to two hands clasping one another and which could clasp and unclasp quickly without endangering the worker. He received a patent for this version on April 29, 1873.

After testing on a local line, Janney convinced a few friends to finance the manufacture of some samples and offers were extended to other railroads. Janney found the railroad men a hard sale. The only one who seemed interested was J. D. Laing of the Pittsburgh, Fort Wayne, and Chicago. He tested the device, found it sound, and began refitting on the Fort Wayne branch passenger cars. At the same time, Laing retained the old link and pin version on the freight line.

Despite Laing's hesitancy in refitting all the cars in his responsibility, the Fort Wayne experiment did lead eventually to the Pennsylvania Railroad adopting the Janney system a few years later. The Pennsylvania was the parent of the Fort Wayne line.

The Pennsy succeeded in having a resolution passed by the Master Car Builders' Association, favoring adoption of the Janney coupler, in 1887. Other railroads were reluctant to go to the expense of refitting cars, expense being more important than the safety of employees.

Thanks goes to Lorenzo Coffin, a part-time minister who had worked on the railroad and witnessed a coupler accident, for making it mandatory. Coffin became a one-man lobbyist for railroad safety. It took until 1893, but Coffin's efforts led to Congress passing the Safety Appliance Act which covered both couplers and air brakes.

President Benjamin Harrison signed the bill on March 3, 1893 and railroads were given five years in which to refit cars to the new specification. Two extensions had to be granted on the deadline.

Coupler injuries dropped from 32 percent to four percent of all railroad injuries in 1900.

SAFETY STOP

The *Danville Morning News* reported June 29, 1903 on the Reading's test of a device the company believed would save lives and prevent costly wrecks.

"The apparatus is an automatic safety stop which will prevent all trains from running past signal boards when the danger signal is exhibited. It will also prevent trains from running into open switches.

"The device by which this is accomplished is of the simplest possible character. There are no pulleys or ropes, which have complicated former inventions of this character. A valve on a projecting rod is placed on a locomotive near the pony wheels. An upright rod on the sills of the road comes into contact with and turns the rod of the locomotive. The air is released by this action and the brake applied, and the train, no matter what its speed, stops within a very short distance and the engineer, before he can proceed, must get out and close the valve.

"Charles Miller, the engineer of Superintendent Luther's 'Black Diamond,' has patented the device and will doubtless make a fortune out of this product of his brain and his long experience as an engineer."

FIRST TELEPHONE TEST

The Pennsylvania Railroad was a pioneer in the use of the telephone in the railway business.

At the company's invitation, Thomas A. Watson, Alexander Graham Bell's assistant, and Gardiner Hubbard, Bell's financial backer, came to the Altoona yards on May 21, 1877 and demonstrated the use of the telephone to Pennsy officials. Impressed with the test, authorization was given to install telephone lines, allowing officials in various departments to communicate by phone. By 1920, the Pennsy was dispatched primarily by telephone.

By the 1950s, the Pennsylvania Railroad claimed to have the largest private telephone system in the world. "Its transmission lines stretch 41,000 miles. Its cost, together with that of the associated teletype network, totals $35 million. On any typical day, PRR lines carry an estimated half-million calls." (*The Pennsy*, March 1955).

DUAL USE

The *Danville Intelligencer* of Friday, March 3, 1905 reported trunk lines of the United Telephone and Telegraph company between Danville and Pottsville, Danville and Shamokin, and other points ". . . are being used simultaneously for telephoning and transmitting messages by telegraph."

The report explained, "The fact that wires could be employed in this dual capacity is a recent discovery. During the past six months, however, the same wires on a few of the railroad lines have been used for both telegraphing and telephoning. As a telephone line, however, the United is among the pioneers in adopting the new method."

Daily, between the hours of 9:00 a.m. and 8:00 p.m., the article said the wires were "hot" with messages by both telegraph and telephone.

"The electrical connection required for using a line for telegraphing and telephoning simultaneously is intricate, but the use of the wire in this way is not expensive and business can be done at less outlay than where a line is maintained for either telegraphing or telephoning exclusively."

VALVE RELEASE

William A. Engle, a Pottsville man, credited a dream for giving him the answer to a vexing problem he faced in inventing a device intended to alleviate delays often experienced in railway travel.

The Danville Intelligencer reported on Sept. 9, 1904:

> In brief terms, the device permits an engine which has been disabled on one side to proceed to its destination by use of the mechanism on the uninjured side. This is accomplished without the disconnection which heretofore has been necessary of pipes, valves and other fittings on the damaged side.
>
> This operations takes from 15 minutes to more than an hour, depending upon the expertness of the engineer and the condition of the locomotive.

Engle, a 16-year employee of the Pennsylvania Railroad, told the *Intelligencer* he had been working on the project for more than a year when the problem he encountered was answered in a dream.

"Concisely stated," he told the newspaper, "my invention consists in providing any desired form of valve for cutting off the supply of steam from one or the other pipes leading to the steam chest. The advantages accruing from the employment of this invention, summed up, are that disconnections under all conditions are entirely avoided and defects in the steam chest and cylinders readily located.

"The usefulness of this valve as an aid to get away when running one sided and stopping on centre is apparent. The value of this valve in setting main valves is that it can readily be determined which side is out."

DEPOTS

The depot, or train station, was a grandiose artistic tribute to the importance of the railroad in its glory days.

Even in the smaller towns, the depot was usually a grand structure unlike most other buildings in a community. Many were designed by the country's most prominent architects, commissioned to create a stunning building that would captivate the viewers with its beauty and functionality for years to come. The original Pennsylvania Station in New York City was designed by the famous architectural firm of McKim, Mead, and White and was considered a masterpiece of the Beaux Arts style. Reading's headquarters terminal in Philadelphia was designed by Francis H. Kimball, designer of the Empire State building among other skyscrapers.

An example of the depots importance to a community is seen by a report in the Nov. 4, 1904 issue of the *Danville Intelligencer* remarking on improvement to facilities of the Delaware, Lackawanna & Western, including the railroad station. The newspaper said, "A railroad station being the first thing noticed by strangers on entering a city, any improvement of a local one should find great public appreciation."

As the railroads failed, many were destroyed. But, the quality represented by these buildings helped fuel a fever for preservation of historic structures. Many have been saved from demolishment and turned to other uses.

The Reading's Market Street Station, for example, has been named a National Historical Landmark and functions today as a market and convention center.

The Harrisburg-Shamokin Express was the first train out of the Reading's new Market Street Station in Philadelphia on Sunday, Jan. 30, 1893.

"It is expected that all the trains now running in and out of the station at Ninth and Green streets will come to the new station in a few weeks," the *Evening Herald*, Shenandoah, reported on Jan. 31.

The Harrisburg-Shamokin train was made up of four cars: "Baggage No. 518, smoker No. 200, passenger coaches Nos. 784 and 686, manned by Fulton Jones, conductor in charge;

Reading freight station. (Courtesy of Larry Deklinski, Delado Photography; Northumberland County Historical Society; and Paul Thomas Studios.)

Daniel J. Harner, baggage master, and Brakemen J. J. Fitch and F. Condor. Engine 356 was held under control by Engineer Michael J. Welsh and the fireman was William C. Orth."

The report said Welsh had been employed by the Reading since 1873 and an engineer since 1887.

The first train into the new depot was the Reading Accommodation, No. 126, drawn by Engine 359, Patrick Cassidy at the throttle; Fireman Frank Gessner, baggage car and five coaches, manned by Conductor Howard Richards, Baggage Master Michael Gillen and Brakemen Horace Baus and George W. Snyder.

Reading's depot on Independence street, Shamokin, was destroyed in 1965 and its freight station was demolished in the next year. The Pennsy station at Liberty and Commerce streets is used for storage.

The Lehigh Valley, at Railroad and Turnpike, and the Reading, at Fifth and Market, both in Mount Carmel, are gone.

Northumberland County has perhaps a dozen depots still surviving. A few are dedicated to civic use, some for

Independence Street station. (Courtesy of Larry Deklinski, Delado Photography; Northumberland County Historical Society; and Paul Thomas Studios.)

Mount Carmel station vintage postcard.

Northumberland depot. (Courtesy of Larry Deklinski, Delado Photography; Northumberland County Historical Society; and Paul Thomas Studios.)

businesses and storage, one as a museum (Turbotville), another as a restaurant (Northumberland).

There are still 26 depots in Schuylkill County. Some are vacant, others have been converted to use for businesses, as residences, and at least three as museums (Irving, Molino and New Ringgold).

For those with an interest, there's an organization, the Railroad Station Historical Society, dedicated to preserving these structures, and it operates worldwide.

STANDARD TIME

"All clocks and watches must be set to conform to the new standard." From a notice in the Nov. 17 *Carbon Advocate* and similar to others in newspapers across the nation. The notice explained:

> From 12 o'clock, noon, of Sunday, Nov. 18th, 1883, the standard time on the lines of the Philadelphia and Reading Company will be that based upon the seventy-fifth meridian of west longitude, and, at the hour named, correct time under the new standard will be given from the office of the Superintendent of the Telegraph at Reading to all telegraph offices.

It was not just the Reading, but all U.S. and Canadian railroads setting the standard adopted on Nov. 18. Rail transportation demanded an efficient and uniform system of setting time.

As people across the country set their time pieces by whatever arbitrary process suited them, there was no standard prior to Nov. 18, 1883. The railroads had their timetables. Yet, if the rest of the world didn't abide by them, the result could be chaos.

Before the railroad, it didn't much matter if people in Shamokin claimed it was 4 p.m. at the same time people in Sunbury said it was 5 p.m. But when you're running a railroad between the two places, you not only want, you need, conformity on the time or there's going to be a lot of angry people.

As early as 1849, the Pennsy had a rule:

Each engineer will be furnished with a watch which will
be regulated by the Station Agent at the commencement of
each trip and must be deposited with him when the engine
returns. If not returned in as good order as it was received,
the Engineer must pay the expense of repairs.

Some communities did make the switch before it became
law. A report in the Feb. 11, 1876 *Sunbury American* said:

The town clock, or the Court House clock, (the proper title
still being in doubt) has been regulated, so as to conform to
railroad time. Better late than never.

Charles F. Dowd came up with the idea of standardizing
time while teaching at the Temple Grove Ladies Seminary
(now Skidmore College) in Saratoga, N.Y. Realizing his idea
had merit, he broached it to a group of railway superin-
tendents and published a pamphlet, "A System of National
Time for Railroads," in which he proposed dividing the nation into four time zones.

While they accepted the use of meridians on Greenwich,
the railroads had their own plan, a system devised by William F. Allen, editor of *The Traveler's Official Railway Guide.*

There was some friction over the railroad's dictatorial
manner and some places were slow in adopting standard
time until they realized its practical value. It wasn't finally
adopted by all until Congress enacted the Standard Time
Act in 1918.

Despite putting the nation on one standard, there was
still one flaw in the system. Railroad crews were expected
to set their watches in conformity. Unfortunately, not all
watches are of the same quality and, until these were all
standardized, there existed the risk of someone going by a
faulty timepiece.

In 1893 the General Railroad Timepiece Standards were
adopted by all railroads.

Regulation of watches used by engineers, conductors, and other critical employees had been practiced earlier, but now it became even more rigid. Railroads appointed time inspectors, usually watchmakers, who decided the make of watch acceptable and set standards for maintenance. The American Railway Association set standards in 1887 and a majority of lines accepted them. Watches were subject to periodic inspection by a certified watchmaker and an instrument that didn't make the cut could keep its owner off the job.

Initially, an acceptable watch was an 18 size, 15 jewel instrument, adjusted to positions, usually up to three. After standards were adjusted by Webb C. Ball, an Ohio jeweler and watchmaker, in the 1890s there was an upgrade to 18-size and 16-17-jewel watches and, by the twentieth Century, it rose to 21-jewel and increase in the adjustment specifications.

Among brands approved for railroad watches were Waltham, Elgin, Hamilton, and Dueber-Hampden. Waltham and Elgin topped the recommended lists by the 1940s.

I have the watches of my dad and grandfather. Both are Elgins.

8

DIESEL DAYS

Some feel the diesel locomotive took the romance out of railroading. For the railroads, its adoption was a means of economy and coping with declining coal shipping revenue and competition with the trucking industry for other freight.

We tend to think of the diesel as a relatively modern innovation. In fact, a precursor of the diesel was tested in England in 1896 based on internal combustion engines intended for railway use and designed in 1888 by William Dent Priestman.

There was a short period when electric locomotives were seen as an alternative to steam locomotives. Baldwin did build several electric locomotives for the Pennsy, which surpassed all others in using this power. The Reading used some electrified locomotives, but only for commuter service in the Philadelphia area. Electrification proved too expensive for most lines.

The diesel engine as we know it was patented by Rudolf Diesel, a German inventor and engineer (U.S. patent date July 16, 1895). Adolphus Busch (co-founder of the Anheuser-Busch brewing company) bought U.S. manufacturing rights from Diesel in 1898. Though Busch dabbled in railroading and other business, he failed to capitalize on locomotive building.

General Electric, which had earlier built an electric locomotive prototype, now entered the scene. By 1917-18, GE had built three diesel-electric locomotives on a design created by Hermann Lemp, an employee. These early models were primarily used for shifting in the yards.

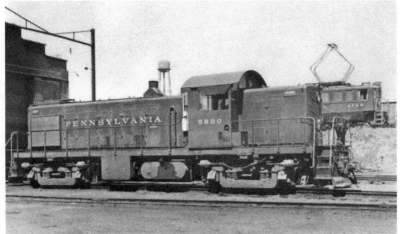

Pennsy diesel. (Courtesy of Larry Deklinski, Delado Photography; Northumberland County Historical Society; and Paul Thomas Studios.)

It wasn't until 1924, in a GE collaboration with Ingersoll-Rand, a diesel locomotive was developed that could handle all normal phases of service for a railroad and cheaper than an electric locomotive.

The first recorded use of a diesel locomotive for switching purposes was in 1925.

The Reading purchased its first two diesels from the American Locomotive Company and put them into service in 1937-38. Between then and 1967, the company would purchase 116 more from ALC and between 1939-53 another 122 from Baldwin.

The Pennsy started adding diesel locomotives in the mid-1940s, purchasing 60 from General Motors and then another 24 from Baldwin. By the late 1950s the PRR had retired its steam locomotives and relied entirely on diesel.

Diesel proved more cost efficient for the railroads, the engines required less maintenance than steam. Some estimates give the annual cost of maintaining a steam engine as 25 percent of the cost of purchase.

Add to this the time and patience it takes to build up the fire for a steam locomotive, the large amount of coal and water required, and the crew needed to operate it and it's easy to see why companies chose to phase out steam. In

Crusader dining car. (Courtesy of Wikipedia Commons.)

contrast to the crew needed for a steam-driven operation, only an engineer and conductor were required in most cases for a diesel.

Some of those passenger trains we remember with fondness were certainly diesels.

Reading's famed Crusader began service on Dec. 13, 1937, the original steam locomotive being replaced by diesel in the early 1950s. The Crusader ran between Philadelphia and Jersey City where a ferry connection could be made to Lower Manhattan. This passenger service was operated in partnership with the Central Railroad of New Jersey. Crusader made its final run on Dec. 3, 1982.

In contrast, the King Coal, which ran between Philadelphia and Shamokin, relied on steam. It was in service from the late 1930s until the last train left Shamokin on June 28, 1963.

The Reading had other passenger lines, including the Harrisburg Special, between Jersey City and Harrisburg, and the Schuylkill, between Philadelphia and Pottsville, as well as the cooperatives with the Central and one with the DL&W, between Philadelphia and Syracuse, New York.

Considering trains in and out of my hometown, Shamokin, the *News-Dispatch* received a letter written by John M.

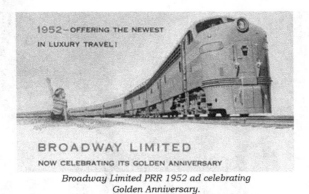

*Broadway Limited PRR 1952 ad celebrating
Golden Anniversary.*

Rolin, who served as a Reading passenger agent in town in the 1930s.[1]

"Mr. Rolin's letter referred especially to 1930, when the Reading Company had nine trains coming into the city on weekdays and eight trains leaving. There were four outgoing and four incoming trains on Sundays.

"Of the eight trains which left Shamokin daily in 1930, seven went to Philadelphia; one, the Williamsporter, had through sleeping cars and coaches from Williamsport to Philadelphia, and similar accommodations to New York, via Tamaqua. The one train which did not go to Philadelphia was a daily trip to Tamaqua, which left here at 1:05 p.m. and arrived in Tamaqua at 3:04."

The Pennsy had a much more extensive passenger service, its web extending over 10,000 miles by the 1920s when it offered hourly passenger service between Philadelphia, New York, and Washington, D.C. Passenger service to those cities had been initiated in the 1880s. One of their more famous trains was the Broadway Limited, offering service from New York to Chicago beginning in 1912 and lasting until 1995 (under Amtrak).

Despite an upturn created by troop and equipment transport during World War II, the writing was already on the wall by the 1940s. The days of the railroad as the preeminent

---

1. My Shamokin, a collection of the Edgar Marlok stories which appeared in the former News-Dispatch, News Publishing & Printing Co., Shamokin, Pennsylvania, 1976

mode of travel and transport were over. Improved highways, more people owning and driving cars, the afore-mentioned competition by trucking, and the advent of long distant bus transportation all contributed their blows to the era of the railroad.

Reading set up a company—Reading Transportation— in 1928 as an addition to rail passenger service. It offered both bus and trucking services, sometimes cheaper options than those the railroad could provide. Bus service covered a wide swath of eastern Pennsylvania. Reading Transportation joined the National Trailways System in 1955, becoming Reading Trailways.

The Reading Railroad sold off its bus routes beginning in 1964. The purchasers were four other operators.

Economic woes forced the Pennsy into a merger with its rival the New York Central in February 1968. The Penn Central filed for bankruptcy on June 21, 1970 and its lines would be split between Amtrak and Conrail.

The Reading also succumbed to bankruptcy in 1971 and its lines were sold to Conrail on April 1, 1976.

9

MISCELLANY

The following is a collection of items which, while interesting, didn't seem to fit into any of the previous categories.

A STRANGE CASE

A former employee of the Philadelphia & Reading Railroad Company who had been discharged for theft and paid back the funds in return for not being charged turned around and sued the president of the company in 1876 for return of the money.

The *Sunbury American* of March 10, 1876 said the jury returned a verdict in favor of the defendant Franklin B. Gowen, represented by S. P. Wolverton.

James M. Pettit, who had been a conductor for seven years, running between Philadelphia and Pottsville, had been discharged after admitting to appropriating company funds to his own use. After being called before Charles E. Smith, then president of the line, and Allen Pinkerton, the detective, he'd agreed to refund $18,000 in bonds in return for not being criminally charged.

Two years later he brought suit against Smith, personally, for return of the funds in Lancaster County Court. Losing that suit, he brought another against the company in Northumberland County, contending the money was obtained from him ". . . by threats of prison or criminal prosecution." Under examination, he swore the bonds did not belong to the railroad company but declined to answer whether he had appropriated company funds.

"The extravagant manner of Mr. Pettit's living created the suspicion that he was rather fast," the *American* said. "It was given in evidence that he sported a four hundred and fifty dollar breast pin, was the owner of a horse that he sold for two thousand dollars, and lived in an eleven thousand dollar house, while receiving a salary not exceeding seventy-two dollars per month."

In rebuttal, the plaintiff claimed he'd been dealing in stocks since 1870 and made profitable "dickers" on watches and chains.

SMOKE NUISANCE

While realizing its importance to the economy, people in towns served by the railroads weren't always happy with some aspects of its presence, as evidenced by an article in the Sept. 10, 1920 issue of *The Call*, Schuylkill Haven:

"Women along Saint John street have oft times protested against the smoke nuisance of engines, whose firemen puddle the fires while lying on the road below the Union street crossing or while going through that section of town. Some of the housewives are convinced that there are some firemen who purposely resort to this means of annoyance especially on wash day. That wash, the interior and exterior of the homes are blackened with this heavy black smoke is quite easily proven."

The newspaper recommended that a formal protest be made to the chief burgess and council.

From the Jan. 28, 1876 *Sunbury American*:

At Lebanon, in this state, Eliza Benson has recovered damages to the amount of $4,250 against the Reading Railroad Company for taking her beyond the station to which she desired to go. The company has taken steps to secure a new trial.

Evening Herald, June 9, 1899

"Reading's New Orders".
The Reading Railway Company has issued an order requiring
train dispatchers to go over the road and familiarize
themselves with the work of trainmen. These jaunts are to be
made whenever possible without interfering with their other
duties. Another notice to trainmen is that they are expected
to fully acquaint themselves with the rules. Meetings of
trainmen will be held and the rules explained by competent
persons.

Juniata Sentinel, June 20, 1877

Vanderbilt's fast train to the west, in its effort to beat Scott's
fast train, ran 150 miles in 184 minutes. We take none of
that kind of riding in our traveling. We'd pull the bell without
orders, get off, and say goodbye, and wait for the next slow
train.

Same paper:

The news agents on the Pennsylvania Railroad have donned
their new uniforms. The suits are made of blue cheviot, and
look much better than those worn by employees on passenger
trains. Each uniform embraces a sack coat, on which are
twelve buttons; tight fitting pants, and caps similar to the
kind worn by Pullman car conductors.

TELEGRAPHY CONTEST

Thirteen telegraphers tested their skills Nov. 24, 1892 in
a contest at Schuylkill Haven sponsored by the *Telegraph
Journal,* a newspaper devoted to news on the service.
    The *Pottsville Republican* of Nov. 25 said G. C. Williams
of Reading won the gold medal and James Hoag of Mauch
Chunk placed second and was awarded a silver medal.
Awards were presented on the basis of the largest number of

words transmitted in a time-limit of five minutes. A typewritten sketch of the life of Thomas Edison was the document used for the contest.

An estimated 200 operators from all over eastern Pennsylvania attended the contest, which was followed by a ball. *The Republican* said Pottsville sent the largest number, followed by Philadelphia and Reading. Judges were C. M. Lewis, Pottsville; E. E. Helms, Pine Grove, and E. A. Kirlin, Schuylkill Haven.

"Superintendent E. R. Adams of the Philadelphia and Reading Telegraph Company provided the keys and outfit for the contest. The Telegraph Journal, under whose auspices the contest was held, will net about one hundred dollars which will be devoted to the improvement of their plant at Schuylkill Haven," the *Republican* said.

Evening Herald, Feb. 2, 1892

The last of the 'Mogul' pattern engines has been retired from service, no one being willing to run it. 'Tis best. Had they been recalled sooner, several lives would have been saved.

BOTH CENSURED

Inquest jurors played no favorites when they ruled in the death of John Dietrick, a Pennsylvania Railroad engineer who was killed in a collision at New Boston Junction.

The *Evening Herald*, Shenandoah, reported on Feb. 3, 1893: "The jury rendered a verdict censuring both the Lehigh Valley and Pennsylvania Railroad companies on account of discrepancies in the rules of the two companies."

Evening Herald, July 21, 1893

Owing to the heavy freight and passenger traffic on the Northern division of the Lehigh Valley, it has been found quite impossible to move coal trains as quickly as desired, and in consequence Coxton yards are crowded with loaded coal cars. It is estimated that fully 6,000 cars, containing about 25,000 tons of coal, are now in the yard.

PECULIARITIES

From a column of "railroad news" in the Jan. 10, 1895
Scranton Tribune:

> Railroaders have their peculiarities in the way of all men:
> Conductor Bennett is great on dominoes, Brakeman Coffman
> is a heavy smoker, Brakeman Patrick Murray is a clever
> carver in wood, Passenger Conductor Charley Nicholls has
> a rare gift of telling humorous tales, Engineer J. R. Troch is
> an apt disciple of Isaac Newton, Conductor E. M. Hallet is a
> first-class hunter, and Conductor Tim Kearney is the heaviest
> man on the road.

My grandfather was a fierce player of dominoes. Dad was
one of the few men in the coal regions who crafted jewelry
from sulphur diamonds (iron pyrite aka 'fool's gold') and
made coal novelties, which he sold as a small supplement
to his income.

A GREAT RIVALRY

The Reading and the Pennsy engaged in rivalry in 1896 over
which line could get a passenger from Philadelphia to New
York in the shortest amount of time.

"The Reading railroad will soon place on the Bound
Brook route, between Philadelphia and New York, a series
of special trains that will make the distance between Philadelphia and New York in 1.05 minutes, which will be fifteen
minutes quicker than the best time now made by any train
between these two great cities of the East," said the *Evening
Herald*, Shenandoah, on March 12, 1896.

"Much of the distance will be traveled at a regular speed
of 60 miles an hour.

"The indications are that the Pennsylvania line will run
a train on competing time between the two cities. There will
be a great rivalry between the two railroad companies and
the traveler will want to go to Gotham in the fastest train."

CHEAP LABOR

The Danville Intelligencer of Sept. 9, 1904 reported on the Reading's employment of Italian immigrants for pennies a day all along its lines but especially on the Shamokin Division, estimating the company had hired about 3,000 and was maintaining each on 10 cents a day or less.

The newspaper lauded the immigrants on their good health and thriftiness.

"Among them there is little sickness and each of them is hale and hearty," the report said.

"All of the men are fresh from Italy, being procured by the agents of the company as soon as they land at Castle Garden. They live in the various towns along the Reading's lines, the company arranging for their sustenance and shelter.

"The padrones (each gang of six to 20 was under supervision of a padron) figure out that it costs about ten cents a day to keep a man.

"Nearly all of the aliens have bank accounts in the towns contiguous to their shacks and the manner in which they accumulate money is, in consideration of the fact that they are paid only from $1 to $1.50 a day, a source of increasing wonder to bank officials."

BROTHERHOOD DAY

A notice in the Friday, July 15, 1904 *Danville Intelligencer.*

Next Saturday will be Brotherhood Day at Edgewood Park, and one of the largest gatherings of railroad men this section has ever seen, is anticipated. Special trains from all over the region will be run to Shamokin.

SNAKE STOPPED PUMP

A large water snake was blamed for idling a Pennsylvania Railroad Company pumping station Saturday and Sunday, July 9 and 10, 1904, south of Danville.

An article in the *Danville Intelligencer* of July 15 said the snake had apparently worked itself into a suction pipe and become snagged in the valve.

"Samuel King, former engineer at the station, was sent up from Sunbury yesterday and was obliged to take the machinery apart. The snake, which was taken out in sections, is said to have been a little less than three feet long and nearly as thick as a man's wrist.

"The pump was idle until late yesterday afternoon, which is a very serious matter where water is in so much demand. Many of the locomotives which usually take water here were obliged to run to Catawissa with the supply they had on hand."

DEPOT BURGLARY

The *Montour American*, Danville, reported Thursday, Nov. 1, 1900 on a "daring burglary" that occurred the previous Saturday at the Philadelphia & Reading depot.

Just after a southbound freight passed the station at 2 a.m., Annon Keiser, night operator, was called to the baggage room window by a voice informing him his friend, Thomas, needed to speak to him.

Keiser said he didn't recognize the voice or know anyone named Thomas. As he raised the shutter, he found himself facing several men pointing revolvers at him. The men entered through the window, bound Keiser, and threw him into the station agent's rear office.

"Before leaving they relieved him of his watch and about $1.50 in money. They also took his tobacco and helped themselves liberally to his lunch. After a number of trials, the safe was finally blown open and the money taken. The amount is not known as the officials have refused to make any statement in regard to their loss. It is supposed to have been quite a large sum, possibly $250."

After the robbers made their escape, Keiser managed to extricate himself from his bonds and raised the alarm. Subsequent issues of the newspaper failed to reveal if the robbers were caught.

RECORD-BREAKING RUN

An AP wire report in the Feb. 21, 1902 *Scranton Tribune* told of the "remarkable time" made by the second section of the Buffalo Express on the Pennsylvania Railroad between Harrisburg and Philadelphia the previous evening.

"The train left Harrisburg at 7:36, arriving here (Lancaster) at 8:12 and had a three-minute stop. Philadelphia was reached at 9:21, making the run of 105 miles in 105 minutes, including the stop here, or an actual running time of 102 minutes.

"The train consisted of five Pullman coaches and was in charge of Conductor Charles Eberly with W. S. Gouller as engineer.

TYPEWRITERS

The Pennsylvania Railroad placed a record order for typewriters in 1902, according to a report in the March 27 issue of the *Middleburgh Post.* The article said the company expected to buy some 2,000 machines to be used by personnel between New York and Altoona.

"All operators now using their own machines will be furnished with a new standard machine to be kept in order by an inspector and repairer who will visit the offices monthly and keep the machines in good condition.

"A number of the local offices have already been equipped with fine instruments. Many of the men, however, still furnish their own typewriters. This big order does not make it look as though the telegraph is to give place to the telephone on the Pennsylvania Railroad."

RAILROAD CONFERENCE

Officials of the P&R and DL&W railroads conferred in Danville in August 1904 on switches and sidings.

The *Danville Intelligencer* of Aug. 19 said, "Much of the carrying done for several of the industries of town involves the transference of cars. It is important, therefore, that the two railroad companies have a thorough understanding in the matter, which naturally involves a full knowledge of switches and the size and location of sidings."

The officials arrived in Danville aboard a special train. Representing the DL&W were T. E. Clark, general superintendent; T. J. Flynn, traffic manager; G. M. Rine, division superintendent; J. B. Keefe, division freight agent; W. B. Hixson, superintendent of bridges and buildings, and J. G. Ray, division engineer.

T. D. Dice, general superintendent, headed the P&R contingent, whose members weren't identified.

WATER SCALE AND TREE FARMS

The *Danville Intelligencer* of Dec. 2, 1904 reported the Pennsylvania Railroad Company had completed the painting of a water scale on the first bridge pier on the south side of the Susquehanna River.

"These water scales appear on all bridges crossing streams along the lines of the Pennsylvania railroad and are intended for observation in times of flood. The company can tell at all times just what danger their property is in at all places."

The newspaper added a bit of advice for the railroad. "In order to procure a uniform scale for the first pier on this side of the river measurements should be procured before the stone workers leave. There is a difference of nearly three feet in the height of the bridge on the Danville side and the exact measurements cannot be obtained from anyone but those who have had the mason work in charge."

The same issue of the newspaper related the Pennsy had purchased five large farms at the mouth of the Juniata River near Clark's Ferry. The report said the railroad planned to plant locust trees on the property with the intent to provide a supply of wood for railroad ties.

"This plan is being carried out by the company at many places adjacent to or near its lines. The company is already meeting with some difficulty in the purchases of railroad ties and they are becoming scarcer each year as more lumber is being cut down."

Hugh Quick of Rupert, superintendent for the Clark's Ferry project, said the company would plant 50,000 trees on the property. He added it would take 20 years for the trees to mature and become fodder for the tie supply.

BOOMING WEIGH SCALES

From the Thursday, May 4, 1905 *Montour American:*

"The Pennsylvania Railroad Company has about consummated a real estate deal at Weigh Scales which means the booming of that village this summer.

"Thursday officials of the company were at the place and laid out plans for the building of additional sidings, a round house, coal dock, and other improvements contemplated this summer.

"The old race track, owned by Mrs. Mary Adams, will soon be transferred to the company and the additional sidings, etc., will run through it."

ARSON SUSPECTED

The P&R sent a railroad detective to Danville on Jan. 25, 1906 to investigate suspected arson of freight cars in the yard of the Structural Tubing Works.

The *Danville Intelligencer* of Jan. 26 said it was only "timely discovery" that prevented the destruction of the car and the possible spread of the blaze to other property of the railroad or the Structural Tubing Company.

The fire was the second of suspicious origin to have occurred in the yard in less than a two-month period.

"Both fires seem to have started in the same way, in one corner of an empty car," the newspaper said. "On the first occasion an empty smoke-stained bottle that had contained kerosene was found in the car. On Tuesday there were no such plain evidences of incendiarism, but it is not doubted that both cars were willfully set on fire, although it is not clear whether the motive was spite or the fire was set by a mere degenerate actuated by a love of mischief. The full problem will no doubt be solved by the detective."

WRECK AVERTED

Two young brothers were credited with preventing a serious accident involving the Pennsylvania Flyer on Feb. 2, 1906 near Nescopeck.

Herbert Parker, 12, and his 11-year-old brother, who was not identified by name in a newspaper report, notified Peter Golden, a trackwalker, they'd seen two older boys tamper with a switch.

The *Danville Intelligencer* of Feb. 9 said the action of the Parker brothers averted ". . . a horrible accident which would have undoubtedly resulted in a large death list."

The boys identified Martin Golden and John McAvoy as the culprits in a hearing before a magistrate in Wilkes-Barre. The two were charged and, in default of bail, remanded to the Luzerne County Prison to await trial.

The trackwalker also testified at the hearing, noting he had been walking down the track toward Nescopeck and saw the two men accused of the crime proceeding up the railroad towards Wilkes-Barre.

"When he neared the switch he was notified by the Parker boys that two men had tampered with it and he at once suspected that the men he saw a few minutes before had something to do with the dastardly work."

BLOCKED CROSSINGS

People in Danville were angry in February 1906 over delays and inconvenience caused by trains blocking crossings for periods of 15 minutes up to a half hour.

"The trainmen are shamefully indifferent, not to say insolent in the matter," the *Danville Intelligencer* said on Feb. 16, "simply consulting their own convenience and refusing to cut a train on the crossing even when requested to do so by people in waiting." The report said drivers had difficulty restraining restive horses and pedestrians often risked their lives by climbing over the cars.

Commenting on an instance the previous Tuesday, the writer said people arriving at the crossing on North Mill street found it blocked by a large P&R coal train. "The crew was engaged in switching cars into the Reading Iron Works. They took their own good time for it and simply ignored the people waiting."

The Reading wasn't the only target for abuse. The newspaper had criticism for the Pennsy also. "The Pennsylvania railroad crews have but little regard for the traveling public and it is no unusual thing for the important crossing there (south side of city) to be blocked for fifteen minutes at a time."

BIBLIOGRAPHY

Coal Catechism. 5th ed. Chapter 13, April 1906.

De Tocqueville, Alexis. *Democracy in America*, vol. II. Vintage Books: New York, 1959.

Donehoo, George P. *The Susquehanna Archaeological Expedition*, second report. Pennsylvania Historical Commission: Harrisburg, 1918, 126-151.

Dyer, William F., editor. *My Shamokin.* The News Publishing & Printing Co.: Shamokin, 1976.

Greater Shamokin Centennial Book, Shamokin, 1964

Greeley, Horace, editor. *The Great Industries of the United States,* J. B. Burr, Hyde & Co., Chicago and Cincinnati, 1872.

Jenkins, Walter Reed. Genealogy Of, Pottsville PA. 1917.

Korson, George, editor. *Pennsylvania Songs and Legends.* University of Pennsylvania Press: Philadelphia, 1949.

Licht, Walter. *Working for the Railroad: The Organization of Work in the Nineteenth Century.* Princeton University Press: New Jersey, 1983.

Meyer, B. H., "Fraternal Beneficiary Societies in the United States," *American Journal of Sociology*, Vol. 6, 1902.

The Outlook Magazine. New York, May 1918.

Sears, Roebuck & Co. catalog, 1900 and 1902.

Various Internet sources

A majority of references are from contemporary newspapers, including:

Sunbury American, Sunbury PA
Philadelphia Ledger, Philadelphia PA
Evening Herald, Shenandoah PA
Shamokin Times, Shamokin PA

Danville Intelligencer, Danville PA
Northumberland County Democrat, Sunbury PA
Shamokin Herald, Shamokin PA
Pottsville Republican, Pottsville PA
Sunbury Weekly, Sunbury PA
Scranton Tribune, Scranton PA
Philadelphia Inquirer, Philadelphia PA
Harrisburg Patriot, Harrisburg PA
The Item, Sunbury PA
Shamokin Daily Dispatch, Shamokin PA
The Call, Schuylkill Haven PA
Carbon Advocate, Lehighton PA
Danville Morning News, Danville PA
Juniata Sentinel, Mifflintown PA
Montour American, Danville PA

ABOUT THE AUTHOR

A native of Shamokin, Northumberland County, Pennsylvania, **J. R. Lindermuth** is a retired newspaper editor who now serves as librarian of his county historical society, assisting patrons with genealogy and research. He is the author of 18 novels and a non-fiction regional history. His short stories and articles have appeared in a variety of magazines. He is a member of International Thriller Writers and the Short Mystery Fiction Society, where he served a term as vice president.
He has two children and four grandsons.

Visit his website at www.jrlindermuth.net